Future Vision, Present Work

Learning from the Culturally Relevant Anti-Bias Leadership Project

Sharon Cronin
Louise Derman–Sparks
Sharon Henry
Cirecie Olatunji
Stacey York

Redleaf Press

Published by: Redleaf Press
                 a division of Resources for Child Caring
                 450 North Syndicate, Suite 5
                 St. Paul, MN 55104-4125

Distributed by: Gryphon House
                 Mailing address:
                 PO Box 207
                 Beltsville, MD 20704-0207

Library of Congress Cataloging-in-Publication Data

Future vision, present work : learning from the Culturally Relevant
    Anti-Bias Leadership Project / Sharon Cronin ... [et al.].
        p.   cm.
    Includes bibliographical references.
    ISBN 1-884834-59-0
    1. Culturally Relevant Anti-Bias Education Leadership Development
Project. 2. Multicultural education—United States—Handbooks,
manuals, etc. 3. Early childhood education—United States—
Handbooks, manuals, etc. 4. Minorities—Education (Early
childhood)—United States—Handbooks, manuals, etc. 5. Prejudices—
study and teaching (Early childhood)—United States—Handbooks,
manuals, etc.   I. Cronin, Sharon.
LC 1099.3.F88   1998
370.117'0973—dc21   98-40490
                                                          CIP

To our children.
S.C.

To Helen Robb, South African activist and anti-bias educator. Gentle
loving warrior, you live on in our hearts and in our actions.
L. D.-S.

To the ancestors for guidance, the creator for my loving family's
support and encouragement, to my mother for her strength and
clarity, and, last but not least, to Leon with thanks.
S.H.

To the early childhood educators, child care providers, and nurturing
parents who work toward implementing the ideas and principles
embodied in the CRAB approach, and to my family for
all of their support during the CRAB years.
C.O.

To my parents.
S.Y.

Contents

Acknowledgments

First and foremost we want to express our most profound appreciation and love to the members of the three CRAB groups. Without them this book would not exist. Their deeply rooted commitment, persistence, enthusiasm, wisdom, and many skills gave life to the work that we called the Culturally Relevant Anti-Bias Education Leadership Project. Their experiences are the realities in which we grounded our writing.

Minneapolis/St. Paul CRAB Group:

Rose Allen
Becky Baker
Kris Barry
Kathy Denman-Wilke
Sue Foster
Joyce Frett
Brenda Fuller
Becky Faust Goze
Barbara Harris-O'Neal
Robin Hasslen
Tracy Hawton
Nancy Johnson
Phalla Keo
Linda Terrell Kos
Mary Loven
Virginia Maldonado
Jeanine Marchessault
Zoe Nicholie
Victoria Rogers
Dorothy Salone
Claire Chang Schroeder
Meg Thomas
Mary Steiner Whelan
Katie Williams
Marcia M. Zeimes

New Orleans CRAB Group:

Cinny Cowan
Cheryl "Olayeela" Daste
Diana Dunn

Barbara Emelle
Margery Freeman
June L. Cataldi Labyzon
Mary L.H. Laurie
Pat Schindler
Bennieta Stansberry
Gail Nelson Swan
Jenni Watts

Also:
William Martin
Sandra McCollum
Kanika Taylor

Seattle CRAB Group:

Sandra Aguila
Nina Aurebach
Margie Carter
Fran Davidson
Kim Statum Francisco
Wendy Dee Harris
Diana Mamerto Holz
Charlotte Fuller Jahn
Theressa Lenear
Ardene Niemer
Dale Otto
Judy Serquinia
Vicki Smith
Janet Beth Staub
Maralyn Thomas-Schier

Gloria Trinidad
Barbara Yasui
Ed T. Yonamine

Also:
Colleen Almojuela
Julie Bisson
Jan Charkow
Marilyn Chu

Micheal Figueroa
Cory Gann
Lynda Joko
Wei Li-Chen
Hadiyah Miller
John Nimmo
Terryl Ross
Kathleen Wolfe

Several others played key supporting roles in our book's journey from conception to birth. We want to express our deepest appreciation and thanks to them. Julie Bisson, the project's grand assistant during the first three years, created and kept the office systems burning. She made it possible for our work to function smoothly. Rheta Negrete Karwin provided sensitive support in the years when this book was conceptualized, written, and rewritten. Our wonderful readers who gave generously of their time and knowledge and helped us see both the value of our work and how to improve it: Claire Chang Schroeder, Barbara Emelle, Andrea Genser, Ed Greene, Mary Pat Martin, Anane Olatunji, Dr. Carol Brunson Phillips, Janet Staub, Carol Young-Holt, and Ellen Wolpert. Dr. Elizabeth Jones provided the structural key to turning our many voices into a coherent narrative that kept our voices clear. Heather Palmer helped us think through how we wanted our book to look and had wonderful ideas about ways to represent our voices visually. Julie Olson Edwards provided additional editorial help that helped Louise solve some knotty problems. Beth Wallace, our Redleaf editor, is a writer's dream. She gave us excellent feedback and respected each of us as authors and as unique human beings. Pacific Oaks faculty supported Louise Derman-Sparks through many years of full time-work on the CRAB project by holding a place for her on the faculty. Deepest appreciation to the A.L. Mailman Family Foundation for providing ongoing financial and collegial support to Louise Derman-Sparks throughout the many years of her work. Thanks also to Dr. Zarus Watson, who provided gentle guidance to Cirecie Olatunji, and to the staff of the Minneapolis Early Childhood Resource Center for their support of Sharon Henry. Finally, a very special thank you to the Kellogg Foundation and Dr. Valora Washington for providing generous, essential funding. From the initial conversations that led to the conceptualization and funding of the CRAB project to its culmination in this book, Dr. Washington remained a steadfast supporter.

Foreword

I have heard that Navajo women and children wear multiple layers of skirts. The layers represent the self, family, clan, community, tribe, and nation. So, too, each of us has multiple identities and needs, and any strategy for social change must consider these many layers of characteristics and opportunities.

This provocative book grapples with the multiple layers of diversity and commonality that we face in the United States of America. The authors, five gifted and courageous women, invite us to witness and share their individual and collective journeys toward culturally relevant anti-bias leadership. Their layers are deep and complex, ranging from self-examination, reflection, and discovery to family interactions to institutional and systems change. At the foundation of their journeys lie unresolved national and global issues of social justice as well as the aspirations of all people.

Many discussions about diversity appeal to our national ideals. We are buoyed by the hope of realizing our country's motto: "e pluribus unum" (out of many, one). We strive for the visions inherent in the Bill of Rights. We recall the power of the resistance movements that have led to undeniable and profound change: abolition, women's suffrage, child labor laws, environmental protection and others. My favorite inspirational message comes from noted educator Horace Mann: "Be ashamed to die until you've won some victory for humanity."

Many discussions about diversity include the change in United States demographics. Between 1995 and 2005, there will be a five percent increase in the portion of the U.S. population under 18 years of age. According to data from Kids Count, however, this increase will not be distributed evenly

across cultural groups for many reasons such as varied birth rates. Also, the number of immigrants in the United States will rise to 9 million in 2010; immigrant children will represent 22 percent of the school age population. Clearly these changes in the racial mix of school children will be reflected later in the workforce as well as in the electorate.

Many discussions about diversity focus on curriculum and teaching techniques. Generally caring and concerned professionals, early educators have strived to be sensitive to the needs of all children. Knowing race to be a "social construct," we are anxious to move on to the business of culturally relevant, developmentally appropriate practice. However, as the authors here quickly point out, many teachers know more about what *not* to do than what can be done; they are often mystified or discouraged by the inevitable confrontations with parents or colleagues who question an anti-bias approach.

Efforts to move from discussions about diversity to systemic change are complex. In my view, change strategies that focus on national ideals, demographics, or curriculum are essential, but incomplete.

How can change occur?

Overcoming resistance is at once profoundly personal, tender, intimate, *and* deeply rooted in social history and context. This book illustrates this dichotomy. As a case study, it demonstrates the exponential power of creating a community of support to nurture our private layers of growth as well as our visions of culturally relevant anti-bias teaching and learning.

With refreshing candor, this book examines both the "unique self" and the cultural experiences that are manifest in each of our lives as we are born, live, work, and breathe in a racist society. Not one of us is untouched, and yet *how* we are affected is in some ways as varied as human life itself.

Willing to reveal their layers and guide us to discover our own, the authors expose the difficult dialogues that can lead to tremendous personal and community growth. For this alone, I offer my gratitude to Louise Derman-Sparks, Sharon Cronin, Sharon Henry, Cirecie Olatunji, and Stacey York.

Yet, as night foreshadows the dawn, confusion, pain, anger, and fear may precede the rewards of doing culturally relevant anti-bias educational leadership, training, and organizing in your own community. It must be clear: the call to action is not a call to guilt, despair, blame, or recrimination. I see the call as an opportunity for assessment and accountability, both personal and professional. This book offers insights both on why the effort to create change is worthwhile, and on how it may be approached.

E pluribus unum. Out of many, one.

Diversity is certain, but unity is the challenge. This book fills me with hope about our ability to find common ground and to transcend our own histories as we influence the next generations' perspectives on diversity.

I hope that you will read this book as part of a group and use it to launch your own community dialogues about how to build a better future in your community, your workplace, and our profession. Reading and working with others can multiply the impact.

I appreciate the work performed by our early childhood care and education colleagues in Seattle, New Orleans, and Minneapolis/St. Paul. Let's all renew and strengthen our contributions to building a democracy that nurtures and treasures us all!

Valora Washington
Kellogg Foundation
August 1998

Preface

This book is written by five women who worked together for five years. Three of us are women of color and two of us are European American. We are mid-career professionals who care passionately about our children and communities. Each of us brings a specific area of expertise to the table: anti-bias education, bilingual education, multicultural education, cultural-identity development, counseling psychology, and community organizing.

Like many women, we struggle to balance dynamic and challenging work lives with even more demanding personal lives. During our time together, we celebrated the birth of two babies and mourned the loss of two parents. One of us got married and became a stepparent, while another sent children off to college. Two of us entered graduate school and earned doctorates, and three of us changed jobs.

Upon reflection we realized that working together as a group allowed us to experience patterns of group dynamics similar to those of the groups we were facilitating. Sometimes we worked in harmony and thought, "We are so blessed to be in the company of these intelligent and gifted women. It is such a gift to be able to spend three days together discussing meaningful topics in a deep way." At other times we clashed like flint and steel, and we would think to ourselves, "I'm never going to work with these people again." Still, we always found ourselves coming back to the table. We continued to struggle together because we had

come to care about one another. We had become committed to one another as well as to the work of culturally relevant anti-bias education.

Our joint work on this book was part of this process of commitment and struggle. We have shaped one another's thinking, although it was never our intent to create one single perspective. We encouraged and respected each other's viewpoints. As a result, this book is written in our individual voices. Each chapter tells part of the whole story in the voice of one or more of the authors and includes anecdotes and thoughts from the others. Through the process of telling the story and the end result—this book—we hope we have been able to model that there can be unity in diversity.

Introduction

The early childhood community in the United States has long grappled with the challenges of diversity and equity in education. Although most early childhood teachers truly want to nurture all children to reach their fullest potential, societal bias has affected programs for young children, as it has other institutions in our society, in both subtle and overt ways. The separation of children by class and race, which often occurs both from de facto segregated neighborhoods and communities and from the separation of funding streams for programs, is an example of the subtle effects of societal biases. The overt effects include the absence of materials that support the home cultures of children of color and the disproportionately small number of people of color in leadership roles in the profession.

For the last forty years, studies and publications have demonstrated the growing evidence of the effect of racism, classism, sexism, and other oppressions on young children's learning processes and their development of strong self- and cultural identities. During the 1950s, pioneering research was conducted on young children's development of racial attitudes. See for example Clark's *Prejudice and Your Child,* Goodman's *Race Awareness in Young Children,* and Trager and Yarrow's *They Learn What They Live.* Based on this research, the "Project in Inter-Group Education" worked in several public school systems throughout the

country between 1945 and 1948 to explore ways to improve interracial and interreligious understanding among children (Taba et al, 1952). Unfortunately this work was not widely known and was nearly lost to future generations because so few early childhood texts included it.

The 1970s saw the emergence of several key books that exposed the racism inherent in the "cultural deprivation approach" to children and families who are not part of the dominant European American culture (for example, Baratz, 1971) and provided alternative culturally relevant approaches, which built on the strengths of the diverse cultures of people of color (Castaneda & Ramirez, 1974).

The 1980s produced several core books about multicultural education. See for example Kendall's *Diversity in the Classroom*. The research of this decade built on the work of the 1950s and produced more information about the importance of culture in children's development and early childhood education. This period also saw the expansion of diversity issues to include gender and class. Key publications of this decade include the following:

Children's Ethnic Socialization by Phinney and Rotherham;

"Bilingualism in Early Childhood" by Garcia (published in *Young Children*);

Alerta: A Multicultural-Bilingual Approach to Teaching Young Children by Williams, De Gaetano, Sutherland, and Harrington;

Non-Sexist Education for Young Children by Sprung; and

"Providing an Anti-Handicappist Early Childhood Environment" by Froschl and Sprung (published in *Interracial Books for Children Bulletin*).

All of this work and more provided the foundation for the growth of the culturally relevant anti-bias approaches of the 1990s, which have gained wider attention and acceptance than in previous decades.

From 1985 to 1989, with the participation of the Pacific Oaks Children's School Faculty, I worked on *Anti-Bias Curriculum: Tools for Empowering Young Children,* a manual that would introduce anti-bias curriculum in early childhood to help educators establish anti-bias and culturally relevant education approaches in their programs. The manual, which was published in 1989, illustrates the harmful impact that preju-

dice and discrimination have on the development of young children, and it reviews the research showing that children notice diversity and begin to absorb societal bias very early in life, even as early as eighteen months. In addition, the book points out that early childhood care and education are not immune to the inequitable and unjust power relationships in society that are based on race, culture, gender, physical ability, sexual orientation, and class. The manual issues a call to early child practitioners to become activists, declaring that "it is not sufficient to be nonbiased (and also highly unlikely)....It is necessary for each individual to actively intervene, to challenge and counter the personal and institutional behaviors that perpetuate oppression." The publication of the *Anti-Bias Curriculum* played a key role in generating increased professional attention to diversity and equity issues in early childhood education and set the stage for the development of the Anti-Bias Leadership Development Project.

From Awareness to Action: The Challenge

After the publication of the *Anti-Bias Curriculum,* I toured the country, meeting with educators, day-care workers, families, and others concerned with the healthy development of our children, families, and communities. I participated in passionate discussions with educators and worked with them to effectively implement an anti-bias approach in their work with children, families, and other teachers. However, it soon became increasingly apparent that most had neither sufficient preparation nor support to do the work they envisioned. Too many teacher preparation programs treated anti-bias work as an "add-on"—a unit within a course or a chapter in a text about child development—rather than as an integral and ongoing part of a child's educational needs. Moreover, the educators' own attitudes and sense of identity rarely were addressed.

Many educators' previous experience with short in-service workshops, which introduce so many early childhood practitioners to diversity and anti-bias issues, had only scratched the surface of anti-bias education.

And, in some instances, these brief, one-shot trainings actually did more harm than good in that they led participants to believe that anti-bias education was simply a matter of acquiring new materials and learning a few new activities. In truth, anti-bias education must go much deeper into the educational process. Unless teachers have guidance, support, and the opportunity to understand the dynamics of institutionalized bias, they are not able to effectively use the anti-bias approach in education.

Although interested in the anti-bias approach, a large number of teachers were wary of using it in their workplaces due to the lack of sufficient support and training. Many educators said they became aware of what *not* to do, but didn't know what, in fact, they could do. Many teachers began changing their classroom environments by adding things such as multiracial baby dolls and books that include a wider diversity of characters but found themselves unable to transform the ways they interacted with children. In some cases, teachers unintentionally distorted ideas from the *Anti-Bias Curriculum* in ways that were harmful to children. Too many teachers did not know how to heed the principle that anti-bias education must be practiced within the context of their students' cultural backgrounds—that teachers should not always use the activities described in the book just as they are, but make choices and adaptations in terms of their own and their communities' cultural experiences and knowledge. Still others found unresolved identity issues within themselves, asking questions like, "How do my cultural roots affect how I work with children?" and "How do I balance my commitment to developmentally appropriate education with the traditional wisdom of my community about how babies should be cared for?" They also uncovered their own prejudices, saying things to me like, "I'm starting to see the class bias in my assumptions. I used to think that kids should wear clothes to school that they can get dirty in, but some people can't afford to buy their kids extra clothes, and they have legitimate concerns about their children being stigmatized at school for being poor."

Sometimes teachers' sincere attempts at incorporating anti-bias approaches resulted in unexpected sparks of disagreement from other staff members or parents. In the face of these types of barriers, even the

most committed teachers felt alone. Many began to question whether they had the courage to face the inevitable confrontations with colleagues and, in some cases, to risk friendships with other staff members as they asked them to look at bias issues in their programs. Some even worried about losing their jobs.

Clearly the anti-bias approach was sounding a deep chord for many people in the early childhood field. Yet the issues involved were so complex and the resistance to change so strong and multileveled that a deeper level of thinking and support was necessary to make it possible for the field as a whole to move toward more equitable programs for children and families.

Why are the issues complex? Where does this deep resistance to change come from? To understand what early childhood culturally relevant anti-bias education means and to move toward equity in early childhood programs, we must pay attention to the larger historic and social context in which early childhood care and education exist. As Carol Brunson Phillips explains in a 1988 article in *Young Children,* cultural diversity is not the root cause of inequity: "Rather than diversity itself, it is the ways in which the major institutions of this country have responded to culturally, racially, and ethnically diverse people that is the major source of social, political, and economic inequality." In order to change early childhood education, then, we must realistically face and address the complex difficulties of building multiethnic collaboration and community in a society with a long and complex history of racism and other forms of prejudice and discrimination, a society which is also founded on revolutionary principles of freedom and justice for all.

This means "unpacking the systemic dynamics—rooted in history and power—that prevent too many children from experiencing nurturing early childhood education." (Enid Lee, speaking at the National Coalition of Education Activists' annual conference, August 1994, Cambridge MA). It means advocating for an inclusive, equitable society in the face of those who do not want such changes to happen. In sum, changing early childhood education to reflect anti-bias and culturally relevant perspectives is not just about changing what we do in our centers, schools, and homes. It is also about transforming the power rela-

tionships in our society and how they are reflected in our deepest beliefs and behaviors in regard to ourselves and others.

From the many discussions I had with educators and others following the publication of the *Anti-Bias Curriculum,* I saw the need for a pilot project that would offer training, leadership, and support for educators committed to tackling the social changes involved in implementing in-depth anti-bias and culturally relevant approaches in education. Through a generous grant, the Kellogg Foundation provided financial support to the "Anti-Bias Leadership Development Project," which eventually became known as the Culturally Relevant Anti-Bias (CRAB) Leadership Project. This three-year project allowed us to form groups of early childhood professionals in three U.S. cities—Minneapolis/St. Paul, New Orleans, and Seattle—in order to develop local leadership and coordinate culturally relevant anti-bias work.

This book is a collection of writings from my perspective as the project director and from the perspectives of the five coordinators of the CRAB groups in these cities. It reflects all of our experiences as well as the lessons of the CRAB project and of anti-bias work in general. Our intent is to provide you with the story of CRAB's development, evolution, and relevance in early childhood education. We hope this manual can be used as a guide to further your own work as an educator in presenting culturally relevant anti-bias approaches in education.

Chapter 1 provides an overview of CRAB's formation, group profiles and activities, and guiding principles. In chapter 2, Seattle coordinator Sharon Cronin gives her perspective on the importance of grounding our work in the history of resistance to oppression. In chapters 3 and 4, Sharon Henry and Stacey York, co-coordinators of the Minneapolis/St. Paul group, reflect on the specific principles, purposes, and strategies of the Twin Cities' CRAB project. In chapter 5, New Orleans coordinator Cirecie Olatunji discusses cross-cultural dynamics within a conceptual framework based on her work with the New Orleans CRAB group.

Chapter 6 discusses issues and strategies to consider when carrying out culturally relevant anti-bias education work in the early child-

hood field, as well as in other communities, based on examples and lessons of the CRAB project overall. Chapter 7, written by the three coordinators of color, recounts the lessons that emerged from the experiences of people of color in the CRAB groups. In chapter 8, Stacey York and I consider the issues facing European Americans involved in anti-bias education work by chronicling the significant points of our journeys toward claiming our identity as anti-racist European Americans. Finally, chapter 9 offers concrete advice for initiating anti-bias and culturally relevant education leadership, training, and organizing in your own community.

Culturally relevant anti-bias education work and community building require constant struggle at many levels; yet, it is this struggle that produces growth, personal healing, strength, and, ultimately, liberation. Though change may be slow and difficult, our work brings closer the possibility that we will one day realize our dream of what bell hooks calls the "beloved community":

> Beloved community is formed not by the eradication of difference but by its affirmation, by each of us claiming the identities and cultural legacies that shape who we are and how we live in the world....We deepen those bondings by connecting with an anti-racist struggle....
>
> —bell hooks, *Killing Rage: Ending Racism*

It would seem that we have come a long way—and in some ways we have. On the one hand, we have clearer direction, principles, and curriculum strategies for creating truly nurturing environments for all children. On the other hand, too many early childhood programs are still talking the talk without walking the walk. For example, throughout the 1990s reports from NAEYC's accreditation process pointed out the fact that scores on the diversity standard continue to be lower than other aspects of the curriculum. The next major phase of the journey to quality care for all is integrating culturally relevant anti-bias approaches into daily practice with children, families, and staff.

Resources

Aptheker, Herbert. *Anti-Racism in U.S. History.* Westport, CT: Praeger, 1993.

Baratz, S., and J. Baretz. "Early Childhood Intervention: The Social Science Base of Institutional Racism." Harvard Educational Review 40.1 (1970): 29-50.

Brunson Phillips, Carol. "Nurturing Diverstiy for Today's Young Children and Tomorrow's Leaders." Young Children (1988): 42-47.

Castenada and Ramirez. *Cultural Democracy, Bicognitive Development, and Education.* New York: Academic Press, 1974.

Cross, W.E. "Black Identity: Rediscovering the Distinctions Between Personal Identity and References Group Orientations." In M.B. Spencer, G.K. Brookins, and W.R. Allen, eds. *Beginnings: The Social and Affective Development of Black Children.* Hillsdale, NJ: Erlbaum, 1985.

Derman-Sparks, Louise, and the ABC Task Force. *Anti-Bias Curriculum: Tools for Empowering Young Children.* Washington, DC: NAEYC, 1989.

Franklin, J. H. *The Color Line: Legacy for the Twenty-First Century.* Columbia, MO: University of Missouri Press, 1993.

Froschl, M., and B. Sprung. "Providing an Anti-Handicappist Early Childhood Environment." Interracial Books for Children Bulletin 14 (1983): 21-23.

Garcia, E. "Bilingualism in Early Childhood." Young Children 35.4 (1980): 52-66.

hooks, bell. *Killing Rage: Ending Racism.* New York: Holt, 1994.

Kendall, F. *Diversity in the Classroom: A Multicultural Approach to the Education of Young Children.* New York: Teachers College Press, 1983.

Lane, J. *All Equal Under the Act.* London: Race Equality Unit/National Institute for Social Work, 1991.

Phinney, J., and M. Rotherham, eds. *Children's Ethnic Socialization: Pluralism and Development,* 1987.

Taba, H., Brady, E. and Robinson, J. *Intergroup Education in Public Schools.* Washington, DC: American Council on Education, 1952.

Williams, L., et al. *Alerta: A Multicultural-Bilingual Approach to Teaching* Young Children. Reading, MA: Addison Wesley, 1985.

Walker, Alice. *The Temple of My Familiar.* New York: Harcourt, 1989.

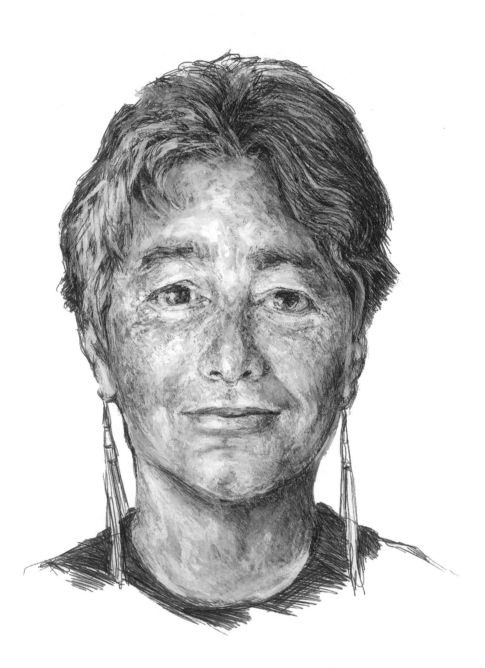

Louise Derman-Sparks
Project Director

Chapter 1

Overview of the Culturally Relevant Anti-Bias (CRAB) Leadership Project

Keep in mind always the present you are constructing;
it should be the future you want.

—Alice Walker,
THE TEMPLE OF MY FAMILIAR

Necessity sparked the initiation of the Anti-Bias Leadership Development Project (later known as the Culturally Relevant Anti-Bias—or CRAB—Leadership Project). It began in 1991, conceived as a way to explore how to meet the many-faceted challenges of making culturally relevant anti bias education an integral part of the daily practice in our early childhood programs. The members of the Anti-Bias Leadership Development Project wanted to explore how we could support change toward anti-bias educational practices within

- ourselves;
- our work with families and staff;
- teacher training and recruitment;
- the early childhood delivery systems for children and families; and
- the policy and infrastructures that define and support quality early childhood care and work.

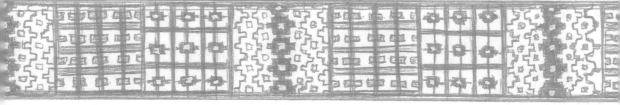

To explore and support the type of change envisioned, I received a grant from the Kellogg Foundation to develop the Anti-Bias Leadership Development Project, which would focus on four major goals:

1. Integrating anti-bias approaches in direct services to children and families;
2. Training other early childhood practitioners and parents;
3. Creating and strengthening policies, infrastructures, and practices that promote anti-bias education within existing early childhood organizations and agencies; and
4. Building ties with other multicultural leaders and with community groups to advocate for new programs and resources.

The purpose of this three-year project was to bring together early childhood professionals in three major U.S. cities to work as a group to develop local leadership for culturally relevant anti-bias work. Minneapolis/St. Paul, New Orleans, and Seattle were chosen as sites for the project, based on their different geographic regions as well as apparent interest and previous experience in educational equity and diversity work.

The guiding premises for the work of the project were originally derived from the four goals of anti-bias curriculum as published in the *Anti-Bias Curriculum: Tools for Empowering Young Children*. Following the principles of anti-bias education would mean that all children experience early care and education environments that

- ◆ nurture children's construction of knowledgeable, confident self-concepts and group identities so that each child can feel confident without feeling superior to anyone else;
- ◆ promote comfortable and empathic interaction with people from diverse backgrounds by guiding the development of cognitive awareness, emotional disposition, and behavioral skills needed to respectfully and effectively learn about differences, comfortably negotiate and adapt to differences, and cognitively understand and emotionally accept the common humanity that all people share;

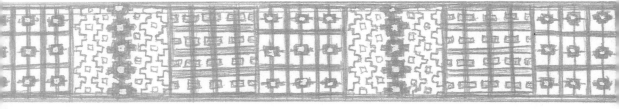

- foster critical thinking about bias so that each individual is able to identify "unfair" and "untrue" images (stereotypes), comments (teasing, derogatory talk), and behaviors (discrimination) directed at oneself or others and have the emotional empathy to know that bias hurts; and
- cultivate individuals' ability to actively resist the harmful impact of biases on their own identity and to take responsibility for standing up for justice when others face bias. This means learning and practicing a variety of developmentally appropriate actions in response to acts of prejudice or discrimination directed toward oneself or others.

In early childhood care and education programs, an anti-bias approach

- acknowledges all of the children's varied racial/ethnic backgrounds, languages, gender, class, differences in physical/developmental abilities and family styles, structures, and experiences;
- weaves cultural and other kinds of diversity components throughout all aspects of the daily curriculum and in developmentally appropriate materials and practices;
- consistently affirms both the similarities and differences among children, while recognizing the influence of misinformation and stereotypes on children's ideas about self and others, and guides children accordingly;
- creates a culture of fairness. Adults point out and help children identify fair and unfair behavior, problem-solve ways to eliminate unfair behavior, and provide information about how people work to change unfair rules;
- provides for personal work on the four anti-bias goals for staff members; and
- includes children's families in a partnership with staff to develop meaningful anti-bias strategies within the program.

The purpose of the Anti-Bias Leadership Development Project as originally conceived was to foster the ability within the early childhood field to provide these kinds of environments in programs for children from birth to age eight.

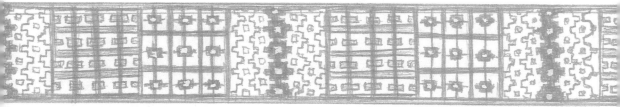

Oppression, Prejudice, and Discrimination

The term *oppression* refers to systemic, institutional forms of power and privilege granted to individuals or a group based on an aspect of human identity (for example, race, ethnicity, gender, class, sexual orientation, and so on). Oppression can be the result of any policy, structure, or action, backed up by institutional power in which the *outcome* accords (1) advantages, privileges, or power to a group of people on the basis of race, ethnicity, language, gender, sexual orientation, class, and so on, and (2) disadvantages to all other groups not sharing in the identity of the advantaged group. For example, oppression based on gender (sexism) accords advantages to men as a group while conversely creating disadvantages for women as a group. Oppression based on race (racism) allows economic, educational, and cultural power to white people as a group at the expense of people of color.

Because it refers to institutional power, the concept of oppression is broader and deeper than prejudice and discrimination. We use the terms *prejudice* and *discrimination* to refer to hurtful or harmful individual acts directed against individuals because of an aspect of their group identity, which may or may not be backed up by institutional power. For example, individual women may be prejudiced against men and may treat individual men badly. However, their actions are not backed up by institutional power, which in U. S. society is accorded to men. Therefore their actions may be examples of prejudice or discrimination but are not examples of oppression, because the outcome of their actions does not accord privilege or power to women as a group, nor does it take it away from men as a group.

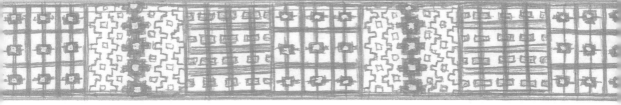

Several beliefs about the nature of doing culturally relevant anti-bias education work guided the initial stages of the Anti-Bias Leadership Development Project. The fuller and deeper meaning of these beliefs became increasingly apparent as we worked together over many years.

1. Culturally relevant anti-bias education requires collaborative effort. We all need the sharing of different voices and experiences to understand the larger picture and where we each fit, to continually analyze and evaluate our work, and to receive emotional support. Moreover, any kind of systemic change requires group power.

2. Our work takes place within a social-political context and history of systemic racism and other forms of oppression. We begin with racism as our starting point for change and then make the connections with the other primary oppressions in our society (sexism, classism, ableism, heterosexism, and so on). This work is similar to a child's kaleidoscope—the elements remain the same but each turn rearranges them in different configurations. We begin with racism because it is not possible to build a just multiethnic community or to work in culturally relevant ways on any issues unless we do so.

> *"Having the CRAB group has given us power. People look up to the leadership in the group so we're opening doors little by little."*
>
> —Seattle CRAB participant

This work requires us to learn about how the systems and institutions in our country operate. It also requires re-educating ourselves about the history of the United States and of the Americas from the perspectives of the indigenous people, the people who were forcibly brought here, and the other groups who have experienced prejudice and discrimination as they attempted to become part of the American fabric.

3. Culturally relevant anti-bias education work must be led by people who are part of and understand the conditions, needs, cultures, and problems of the people in their city and various communities. This

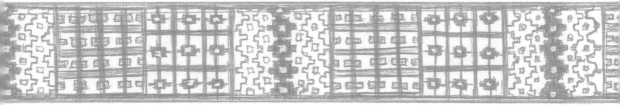

8 Ethnicity, Culture, and Race

The concepts of ethnicity, culture, and race are complex and deserve greater discussion than this manual can cover. (For detailed discussions on these concepts, see the suggestions for further reading in the appendix.) Since these concepts are often erroneously used interchangeably, we have included here brief definitions to use as references with this text.

Ethnicity

Ethnicity is the geographic origin or national identity of a person. For example, the terms *African American, Irish American,* and *Mexican American* identify a person's ancestral, national, or geographic identity. The term *Latino* includes people from many countries, such as El Salvador, Nicaragua, Mexico, Puerto Rico, and so on. The term *Native American* includes a wide range of tribal groups, each with its own language and way of life.

Terms such as *Cherokee, Hopi,* and *Lakota* refer to more specific ethnic identities, which in this case are Native American tribal affiliations. A person's ethnic identity cannot be assumed from physical traits. Two people with similar skin color, for example, may be from two different ethnic groups, and yet two people with very different physical characteristics can come from the same ethnic group.

Culture

Culture is defined by the values, traditions, social and political relationships, and worldview shared by a group of people bound together by a combination of factors that include one or more of the following: a common history, geographic location, language, social class, and religion. Culture is learned, not inherited.

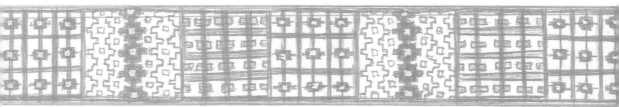

Race

The American Heritage Dictionary defines race as "a local geographic or global human population distinguished as a more or less distinct group by genetically transmitted physical characteristics." A more accurate definition for our purposes derives from *All Equal Under the Act* (1991): "...the unacceptable categorization of peoples in biological terms constructed to aid the justification of the systematic oppression of people of color and create an ideology of racism." The concept of race emerged in the eighteenth century, when Europeans began claiming land in Africa, Asia, and the Americas. Accredited scholars in anthropology, biology, and, later, psychology, as well as politicians and religious figures, helped formulate the idea that human beings could be categorized into different biological groups based on their physical appearance, especially skin color. For the next two centuries, various scholars and scientists claimed evidence that "Caucasians" (as they called European people) were not only biologically distinct from other races but also the most advanced biological group within the human species. They also argued that "Negroids" (as they referred to African people) were the least advanced.

Though biological inferiority or superiority has never been proven, it also has been impossible to establish any biological criteria for defining race itself. Still, most people have come to accept the concept of race as if it refers to an objective biological reality.

idea is eloquently expressed by one CRAB group member's reflections on the meaning of leadership:

> "I have always resisted the word *leadership* because I think the idea that gets pushed in the dominant culture is of someone who takes charge, who gives orders, who directs people. That is something that I never felt comfortable with. So, whenever I heard the phrase

'be a leader' or 'take leadership' I always had this sour taste in my mouth. From my cultural perspective, if one goes ahead, we all go ahead. So, leadership means sometimes I may be up front calling everyone to come with me. Or I may be at the back pushing people forward. Or it may mean that we are standing side-by-side holding hands while we're walking together. To me that is what leadership is all about. So in the sense of this project, I have become a leader, by my definition. And it has actually been wonderful to be able to say that there are different ways of leadership."

—Seattle CRAB participant

4. Our work is part of a long history of resistance by people from all ethnic groups sustained over many generations. Most of us lack knowledge of this history. Our school education rarely addresses it in any more than a very limited manner, if at all. Nevertheless, it provides inspiration and lessons for our own work today. We must uncover and learn the stories of this resistance in our own cultural groups and among the communities whose children and families we serve, and then connect our own efforts with it. We must also uncover the larger picture of struggle that has occurred and continues to occur in our nation to build a truly democratic, pluralistic, and just society.

> "The changing of values and ideas is what's going to change the whole structure. It has to be a personal change or it's not going to happen."
>
> —Seattle CRAB participant

5. Doing culturally relevant anti-bias work requires growth at the personal level as well as in skills for creating professional and systemic change. Action without personal growth is an invitation to contribute to the problem one is trying to solve; however, personal growth without taking action in one's various communities becomes self-indulgence.

This process requires, to one degree or another, unlearning previous beliefs about our cultural identity, our educational institutions, our society's history. It requires uncovering and confronting our own ideas, attitudes, and behaviors that collude with and perpetuate racism and other forms of oppression. It further requires constructing new perspectives and a sense of identity

People of Color and White People

People of color is a general term that includes all of the different national or ethnic groups with the exception of European Americans, such as African Americans, Asian-Pacific Americans, Latino and Puerto Rican Americans, and Native Americans. This term encompasses all the specific ethnic groups that are targets of systematic racial oppression.

White people is a general term that refers to members of all the different national and ethnic groups of European origin who emigrated to the United States. Culturally, white people in the United States trace their origins to one or more specific ethnic groups in Europe. The term *European American* is often used when referring to the cultural identity of white people. The concept of white people comes from the political construct of race. It is used to discuss power relationship dynamics and issues that are derived from the institutional system of racism. As a group, white people have come to control and benefit from the economic, political, cultural, educational, and legal institutions in the United States. However, white people as individuals do not equally control or benefit from these institutions. Factors such as ethnicity, class, gender, disabilities, and sexual orientation affect *the degree* to which an individual experiences the benefits of being white.

and practice. We must gain the knowledge and skills necessary for creating systemic changes in the practices of early childhood care and educational programs, teacher training, and city and state policy-making.

6. A learning community where group members actively teach and learn from each other creates the environment for fostering and sustaining the self-understanding, knowledge, and skills required to do culturally relevant anti-bias education. In a learning community, participants

> *"As white people in the group, we are having to deal with issues of power and agenda, and those are things that we white people were really oblivious to at first. We were so concerned with getting out there and training other white people. We were taken aback to find out that we were still kind of running the show. So there have been a lot of humbling times during this, and I think that produces growth."*
>
> — Minneapolis/St. Paul CRAB participant

use their life experiences as the starting place. As multiple perspectives are revealed, each person begins to understand better who she is and where she fits into a much larger picture. This material provides the "raw data" for group members' reflection and analysis, and it leads to new practice both within the group and in the surrounding community.

7. A multiethnic learning community is a living microcosm of the complexities of building effective multicultural working relationships. Creating and sustaining an equitable multiethnic learning community requires undoing the power relationships of racism and creating a multicentered, instead of a Eurocentric, orientation and agenda. From the vantage point of hindsight, and as a result of analyzing our experiences with the CRAB groups, we came to call this vital process "moving the center." Moreover, effective examination and action on other aspects of oppression (for example, class or heterosexism) is not possible unless the power relationships of racism are challenged and changed within the group.

8. Work toward personal growth and systemic change is a lifelong journey. The CRAB approach prepares us for the long haul. Individuals came to the CRAB group at various stages of the journey and continued growing from there. By engaging in personal growth through the building of a learning community we began to heal ourselves of the damage inflicted by racism and other oppressions. In doing so, we also developed and strengthened our ability to work together to create educational and social change.

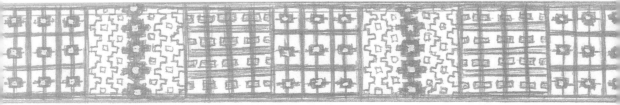

Implementing the Project

In developing the Anti-Bias Leadership Development Project, I anticipated that the project's strength would stem from the groups' operating as informal networks of people who work within the various early childhood programs, colleges, agencies, and organizations. I hoped this networking infrastructure would help each group member to understand more fully the scope of changes that would be necessary to achieve the kinds of sweeping changes demanded by the project's goals. I also hoped it would open up possibilities for creative strategies across programs. I wanted each group to be formally independent of existing early childhood agencies and organizations to prevent the project from being viewed as a representative of a particular agency in the community.

Each group would comprise a coordinator and fifteen to twenty-five people working together on the project's four goals. Participants would include people from the various arenas of early childhood work: teachers of young children, parent educators, teacher trainers, college faculty, staff from resource and referral agencies, program administrators, city and state agency staff, and activists and leaders in early childhood organizations and community advocacy groups. Each group would also be multiethnic, with members representing the various ethnic/cultural backgrounds within each city.

The coordinators and I would also recruit group members who had professional experience in the areas of gender equity, disability rights, gay and lesbian family rights, inter-

"Being in the women of color 'caucus' of CRAB really helped me understand and better deal with the reality of the racial power relationships. Here's an example: Early on, several of the white people in our group were ready and in a position to begin initiating some systemic change at the state level. Their agenda didn't fit for me, and yet they were doing it in the name of dismantling racism. The women of color group helped me see that the problem for me was that the white people were on their own time line, not mine, or many of the other women of color in the group. With us as people of color, you can't just say "be ready" and then expect people to be ready. You can't force readiness—you have to do the trust part. If you do things too fast, sometimes you end up in a worse place than where you started."

—Minneapolis/St. Paul
CRAB participant

racial/ethnic family support, and ethnic-specific advocacy groups. These individuals were important to our project because they already had experience in equity and diversity issues, upon which they could develop the skills necessary to become trainers, organizers, and advocates in their various arenas of early childhood work.

Each participant would need to commit three years to the project. This commitment would allow enough time for each member to build the knowledge base and skills necessary to do culturally relevant anti-bias educational and community work, to provide support to one another, and to work to create change in relation to the project's four goals.

To find coordinators to set up and facilitate each city's group, I sought individuals known and respected in their communities as leaders in diversity and equity work and with strong connections to the early childhood community. All four of the women (Sharon Cronin in Seattle, Cirecie Olatunji in New Orleans, and Stacey York and Sharon Henry in Minneapolis/St. Paul) drew upon their many connections to people in the early childhood community and in diversity and anti-racism work to launch the project groups.

Initially the project was called the "Anti-Bias Leadership Development Project." However, Sharon Cronin suggested that the name should be changed to acknowledge the long history of work by people of color in establishing a decisive voice as to how their children are cared for and taught. She proposed adding the term "cultural relevancy" to the project's title to clarify the fundamental connection between the concept of providing programs for children of color that support and reflect their home culture (thus, "culturally relevant" environments) and the anti-bias goals as they were originally formulated. We adopted the name "Culturally Relevant Anti-Bias Leadership Project" (CRAB, for short). In addition, we added the following to our list of anti-bias goals: "Guide children to develop biculturally so they can effectively interact within their home culture and the dominant culture."

As it often goes with anti-oppression work, agreeing on the name was relatively easy. In theory, we all supported the acknowledgment that children of color and European American children have different cul-

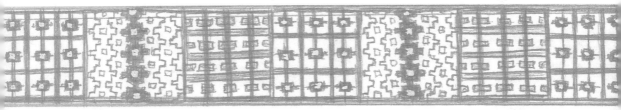

tures, experience different challenges to their development, and come from communities with different histories. However, as you will learn in subsequent chapters, understanding and practicing the intricate dance between the two fundamental concepts of cultural relevancy and anti-bias work was complex and not easily accomplished. We all had to confront the ways in which bias was still active in our lives and in our work with each other to fulfill the promise of our project's new name.

The Coordinator's Role

The CRAB group had a two-way accountability—to its members and to the early childhood and community people with whom the group worked. It was part of the coordinator's role to balance these responsibilities. Key to effective and responsible functioning was the skilled leadership of an individual or two (intercultural, if possible) with experience in early childhood and diversity issues.

Tasks of the CRAB group coordinators included:

- setting up the CRAB group (advertising, recruitment, selection of participants);
- planning and facilitating monthly meetings (over time, planning and facilitating tasks were increasingly shared with group members);
- planning training retreats, with input from group members, and co-facilitating them with me, the project director;
- functioning as contact person and coordinator for training requests from the local early childhood community;
- providing technical assistance and support to group members in their work;
- building connections with other active players in diversity and equity in their cities; and
- networking with other CRAB group coordinators for exchange of ideas and methods, ways to remove problem-solving barriers, and providing support for the emotional challenges of the coordinator's role.

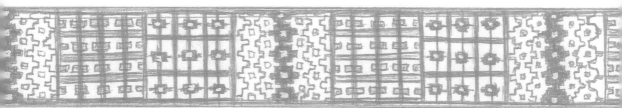

The Minneapolis/St. Paul CRAB Group

The Twin Cities' early childhood community has considerable experience in advocating for innovative programs and supportive governmental policies. The metro area, like Minnesota as a whole, is 92 percent European American. As of the 1990 census, however, the cities of Minneapolis and St. Paul had, respectively, 21.6 percent and 17.7 percent populations of people of color. In addition, Minneapolis/St. Paul has the fourth fastest growth rate in the nation of African Americans, Hispanic/Latino Americans, and Asian/Pacific Islander Americans. The Twin Cities are also home to people of the Anishinabe, Lakota, and Dakota Indian nations.

The Minneapolis/St. Paul CRAB group consisted of 28 people, including twelve women of color (African American, American Indian, Latina, and Asian American—Chinese and Vietnamese) and sixteen European American women, one of whom was visually impaired.

Group membership represented the following professions in the early childhood field:

- Eight teachers (child care, preschool, after-school care)
- Five parent educators
- Three early childhood center directors
- One Head Start education coordinator
- One director of a center for children with special needs
- Three staff members (including one director) of resource and referral agencies
- One staff member from the Minnesota Extension Service
- Two faculty members from four-year colleges
- One staff member from the State of Minnesota Department of Human Services

Recruiting Group Members

To find members for the groups, we informed as many early childhood care and education practitioners as possible, including individuals not active in the obvious early childhood networks and organizations.

Each local coordinator sent recruitment flyers to all early childhood programs and agencies, as well as to community groups and individuals with special interest in diversity and equity education work in their respective cities. Each local coordinator also directly recruited people she thought might be interested in the project and depended upon word of mouth advertising, as well. All of our communications provided necessary information about the group's purpose and requirements and explained that the group would be a place for participants to grow and enrich one another by learning and working together. Some flyers included endorsements from respected early childhood organizations, as well. In New Orleans, for instance, the flyer mentioned that the project was endorsed by the Louisiana Association for the Education of Young Children and several other community organizations.

Our recruitment challenges were similar to those faced by many early childhood programs and organizations seeking diversity. Despite our attempt to spread a wide net, our main strategy of mailing and posting flyers seemed to work best for recruiting European Americans. Word-of-mouth recruitment by respected individuals was critical for enlisting people of color. Sometimes we had to do additional recruitment after the group was formed. In Minneapolis/St. Paul, for instance, we began with only six applicants of color. This may be close to the actual proportion of people of color in the population, but when we met for the first training intensive, the group was unhappy about the overwhelming majority of European Americans within the group. Consequently, group members took a major role in a second round of one-on-one recruitment, and six more people of color then joined.

In New Orleans we had another challenge in recruiting applicants reflective of the city's diversity. Though we received a sufficient pool of African American applicants, we did not receive applicants from other

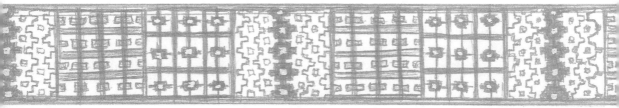

⊞ The Seattle CRAB Group

Seattle has a diverse multi-ethnic population. Networking among the various early childhood care and education agencies was already in the organizational process when CRAB began. A local innovative 1991 conference, entitled "Children, Race, and Racism," helped to prepare the early childhood community for the beginning of the CRAB group.

The Seattle CRAB group consisted of twenty-one people, including ten people of color (American Indian, African American, Japanese American, and Latina), several of whom were bilingual, and one of whom was a man. The group also included nine European Americans, three of whom were Jewish, and one of whom was a man.

Group membership represented the following professions in the early childhood field:

- One family day-care provider
- One bilingual elementary school assistant teacher
- One parent educator
- Two Head Start staff members (center director and multicultural coordinator)
- Three early childhood center directors
- One education coordinator from the Washington State Early Childhood Education and Assistance Program (ECAP)
- Four staff members from resource and referral agencies
- Four faculty members from community colleges
- One faculty member from a four-year college
- Two Childcare Specialist/Childcare Center Licensers from the state

populations of color, which may reflect the lack of ties between the African American community and other "minority" groups.

In Seattle the local coordinator, Sharon Cronin, used her community and professional ties to successfully recruit other people of color. Sharon found it critical to be clear that the CRAB project did not want to impose a "white" way or only one way of addressing diversity and equity issues.

Our recruitment experiences taught us that considerable preparation must precede actual recruitment. The CRAB project's explicit purpose to create change in early childhood work nevertheless walked in the long shadow of the institutional and individual racism that people of color have experienced both from and within the field. Consequently, we found that many people traditionally underrepresented in the field did not easily or initially trust the CRAB project's efforts at social change, especially those people who are underrepresented in leadership positions or those whose cultures or languages had not been respected. From this experience we learned that it was essential to talk with people of color and other underrepresented groups about the project and their needs and concerns before setting up the CRAB groups. This informal discussion took place over time and ensured that the groups would meet their needs and gain their participation.

The profiles of the three groups, which appear in boxes on these facing pages, identify the players whose experiences are the basis of this book. Naturally, during the course of each group's years together, one or two people left the group, and some individuals changed jobs. These lists reflect the sum total of the individuals involved in the CRAB groups throughout the project. The makeup of each group is reflective of its community. Thus, if you were to form a CRAB group in your community, its make-up would reflect your area's demographics and needs and would not be identical to any of those outlined in our project.

Selection of Group Members
To choose CRAB group participants from among those interested in the project, we had each potential member fill out a written application. Applications were sent to anyone who requested one. Working with

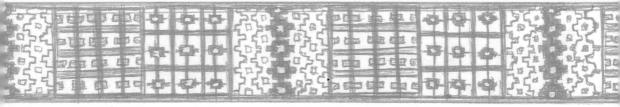

☷ The New Orleans CRAB Group

New Orleans has a majority African American population. European Americans make up the next largest population within the city, with smaller numbers of other groups of color also represented. African American and some European American parents, joined by educators within the early childhood and primary school community, have been struggling for many years to make education programs more responsive to the needs of African American children. Despite the majority of people of color in the city's population, leadership in the more traditional early childhood organizations has tended to be European American.

The New Orleans CRAB group consisted of thirteen people, including six African American women and seven European American women.

Group membership represented the following professions in the early childhood field:

- Two teachers from the University Children Center
- One director from the University Children Center
- One primary school teacher
- Two parent educators
- One director from the Ecumenical Child Care Network
- Two staff/teacher trainers from the state child advocacy and resource and referral agency
- Two staff members from the New Orleans School District department of Early Childhood Curriculum and Instruction
- One anti-racism trainer from the People's Institute for Survival and Beyond

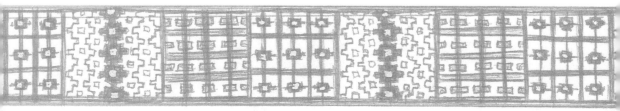

those returned, the local coordinators and I made selection decisions. The application included questions that would enable us to find people demonstrating:

- background in child development and early childhood education;
- experience working with children or adults on diversity or equity issues;
- introspection about their identity and responsibility for participating in the work of gaining social equity;
- awareness of the existence of institutional racism and other forms of institutional oppression in our society; and
- commitment to the group for three years and to working within their communities and the early childhood education field.

> *"The work I've seen coming out of the CRAB leadership groups is very powerful because the participants are able to sustain their energy and belief that they can make things change and that things can really change. The group support makes that possible."*
>
> —Carol Brunson Phillips

The application also included questions related to an individual's professional experience, personal journey, and leadership experiences, including the following:

- Describe your past as well as current work experiences and how you addressed diversity and equity issues.
- What personal issues have you dealt with in the past and what are your current personal challenges/struggles related to your diversity work?
- Describe your personal journey in coming to understand/accept your ethnicity/culture and other aspects of your identity.
- What kind of leadership have you provided in your community-at-large, and in the early childhood education field in general, in relation to diversity/equity issues? Include names of early childhood and community organizations in which you are active.
- Why do you want to be a part of the CRAB project? How will this experience fit into your life and professional goals?

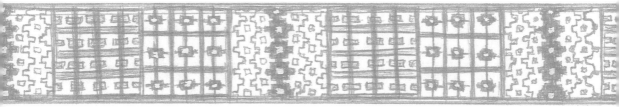

The written applications were very useful to us as a basis for selecting group members. Several applicants later remarked that although the application process was time-consuming, they felt it had been a worthwhile effort because it caused them to think deeply about their feelings concerning the issues involved.

In a few cases, the coordinators and I interviewed individuals in place of the written response. However, in the future we would use a more multifaceted strategy. The written application, although tremendously useful to the organizers, automatically screens out people who, for whatever reason, are less comfortable with completing a detailed form in written English. Adding the option of an interview thus widens the pool of applicants.

CRAB Group Tasks

Each CRAB group made its own decisions about how to work on the CRAB project's overall goals and the activities that would be most appropriate to the community. Yet, the structure for this work was uniform throughout. For the two-and-a-half to three years of the project's duration, monthly group meetings in each city provided opportunities for group members to brainstorm, to examine possibilities for taking action, and to receive ongoing support for one another's work. Group members held the four- to five-hour meetings at their work sites, homes, or in other community meeting spaces. Two of the groups held meetings during work hours since group members were able to get release time, and one group met after work in the late afternoon or evening. Each group also held a twice-yearly, three-day retreat at low-cost conference centers. In instances where time off from work was a financial problem for a member, the groups provided financial support for substitute staff at the member's workplace. Some groups also paid for child care during meeting times.

The scope of each group's internal work

The self-development of the participants in the CRAB groups was one of the major functions of the monthly meetings and twice-yearly retreats. To this end, each group engaged in mutual learning on a range of topics, which were chosen by each group's coordinator and members, emerging from each group's sense of where members needed to grow.

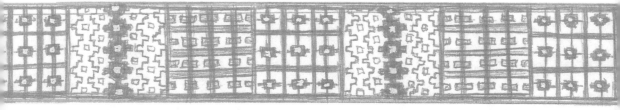

Over time, each group explored similar topics, but the sequence and amount of time given to any particular topic varied.

The training retreats for all three groups covered the same topics. The first retreat focused on examination of institutional racism and the social-psychological impact on group members' cultural identity development. During the second year, the retreats focused on child and adult development and adult training methods. During the third year, the retreats focused on the group members' outreach work, examination of other oppressions (for example, ableism or heterosexism) and methods of dealing with organized opposition to anti-bias education.

The scope of each group's community work

The activities undertaken by CRAB group members were self-determined, keeping in mind the overall CRAB project's goals. Activities in individual group members' workplaces were determined by each member and included the following:

- ◆ Bringing anti-bias approaches into direct work with children, including the work done in family day care, child development centers, kindergarten/grade 1, YWCA child care, and school district after-school care programs.
- ◆ Exploring culturally relevant strategies with parents and introducing anti-bias topics in early childhood and family programs in Minneapolis/St. Paul, to school district parent groups in New Orleans, and to a support group for parents of Deaf children in Seattle.

Common Topics for Monthly Meetings:

Cultural Identity ◆ Cross-cultural Communication ◆ Anti-Semitism ◆ Developmentally Appropriate Practice ◆ Racism ◆ Culturally Relevant Early Childhood Programs ◆ Ageism ◆ Stages of Adult Identity Development ◆ Adult Education Methods ◆ Sexism ◆ Anti-bias Curriculum ◆ Internalized Oppression ◆ Culturally Specific Parenting ◆ Heterosexism ◆ Parent Empowerment and Education ◆ White Privilege ◆ PolicyDevelopment ◆ Social Systems ◆ Community Organizing ◆ Being a Leader ◆ Advocacy Work in Organizations ◆ Ongoing Analysis of Local Needs of Children and Families ◆ Ongoing Analysis of the Early Childhood Community ◆ Bilingual/Bicultural Early Childhood Programs

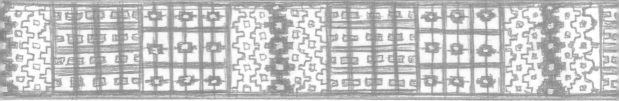

Examples of Application Responses

In reviewing the applications of potential project participants, we especially valued those responses that indicated personal reflection, desire for further growth, and a recognition of responsibility for participating in personal change and change within organizations and society. Here are a few particularly insightful examples:

- I am an enrolled member of the Blackfeet Tribe. I attended both reservation and nonreservation schools. I have experienced what it is like to be stereotyped and misunderstood. I have also seen what helping teachers can do to create changes in attitudes.

- This project is an opportunity to gather all thirty-plus years of experiential growth as a man of Okinawan-Hawaiian background into a conceptual and focused framework. I see it as a chance to verbalize the struggle to identify my culture, to define my maleness and the acceptance of becoming human. Diversity and equity issues affect the core integrity and dignity of each human being.

- I still mourn the "whitewashing" of my cultural roots, the lack of diversity and the racist practices of my growing-up years. I have had to overcome the feeling that I was the victim of my white forefathers' actions and find out what responsible action I could take. I am now more comfortable with the belief that white people can and should participate in this work. What matters is the approach and our ability to listen and inform ourselves.

- I am clear about and proud of my African American identity. I am in the process of examining and struggling with my beliefs about sexual orientation, the women's movement, and interracial relationships. This is one of my reasons for applying to the CRAB group.

- Generally, I have felt more comfortable working in diverse groups of people. Although I am European American, in the past I have shied away from dialoguing with other European Americans in an ongoing way—I guess from the underlying assumption that I had less to learn from them. Also, I am not consistently rooted in my own cultural community. This is an area I want to work on.

- I have always accepted my African American ethnicity. However, I had not always known or acknowledged the whole African history, culture, and heritage of my ancestors. I want to help other people of color become more knowledgeable and accepting of their own histories and cultures. In addition, I want them to understand how institutional racism works and to learn how to address other issues of diversity and equity.

- Creating new courses and integrating anti-bias topics into early childhood courses in community and four-year colleges. In Seattle, this included several CRAB members' setting up and working with their early childhood department committees to rewrite the whole curriculum to be more inclusive, relevant, and committed to anti-bias principles.
- Setting up cultural diversity committees and initiating staff training and work on new mission statements, recruitment and hiring policies, and more collaborative ways to work with parents.
- Integrating culturally relevant anti-bias ideas into licensing requirements in Seattle and in state early childhood policy in Minnesota.

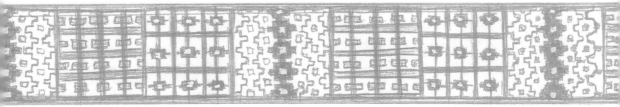

- Integrating CRAB ideas into the work of resource and referral agencies in all three cities, using a variety of activities. In Seattle an anti-bias teacher's support group was established as part of a teacher training program. Group members met with the cultural diversity committee of the Minneapolis Day Care Association to discuss coordinating Latina and South East Asian outreach efforts between MCDA and Child Care Resources.

The activities above were largely carried out by individual group members. CRAB group members also collaborated on work in the early childhood communities in their cities. In-service teacher training was one major type of activity. Much of this work was initiated by requests from various programs and agencies in each CRAB group's city and region. This training ranged from specific workshops on particular culturally relevant anti-bias education topics to integrating these perspectives into other early childhood subjects. (For example, I weave these concepts into the in-service classes I do on developmentally appropriate practices and conflict resolution for early-childhood-education public school teachers in New Orleans.

Collaborative work also took place within each group's local and state early childhood organizations. For example, activities within each CRAB group's state Association for the Education of Young Children (AEYC) affiliates included:

- working on all three state AEYC conference committees to increase workshops on relevant topics and to set up regular diversity/equity conference tracks;
- diversifying the leadership of Washington AEYC by 300% by organizing to elect people of color to the state board of directors; and
- writing for affiliate grant proposals from NAEYC to help programs in Washington implement the "Cultural and Linguistic Diversity" position paper.

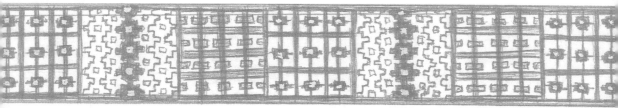

From Idea to Reality

A.A. Milne, the wise author of the Winnie-the-Pooh children's books, has one of his characters muse, "When you think about Things, you find sometimes that a Thing which seemed very Thingish inside you is quite different when it gets out in the open and has other people looking at it." In a similar way, the CRAB group's approach evolved from its initial vision and framework as the participants in each CRAB group grappled with the complexity of creating change in themselves, in their interactions with each other, as well as in their workplaces and community. In his final report to the Kellogg Foundation, the CRAB project's evaluator, Regie Stites, wrote:

> It is very difficult to separate the professional and personal impact of the CRAB experience. Evidence of personal growth and professional activism among project participants is inextricably intertwined. In a fundamental sense, the path taken by each participant was unique. On the other hand, there were a number of points at which the path of most, if not all, participants converged:
>
> 1. The experience of working with others within the context of the group provided participants with many insights into the limits and potential of multiethnic, multiracial collaboration on anti-bias issues.
> 2. Being part of a group of people who take this work seriously solidified many members' commitment. The support received from other group members allowed many participants to speak out in contexts in which they might not have felt comfortable doing so in the past. In one way or another, nearly everyone I spoke with expressed the sentiment that the work once taken up cannot easily be put aside.
> 3. The group experience and training gave participants insights into sources of resistance to anti-bias education and has provided the resources (often other group members) and the knowledge (for example, recognizing that change is a long-term process) to help members deal with the fear and anger they often encounter in their work.

In sum, we learned, as many people have before us, that a group made of people committed and accountable to each other over time makes change happen—in themselves, in their work, and in their community. Each of us brings only a piece of the puzzle, and the whole is indeed greater than the sum of its parts.

Resources

Aptheker, H. *Anti-Racism in U.S. History.* Westport, CT: Praeger, 1993.

Franklin, J.H. *The Color Line: Legacy for the Twenty-First Century.* Columbia, MO: University of Missouri Press, 1993.

Lane, J. *All Equal Under the Act.* London: Race Equality Unit, National Institute for Social Work, 1991.

Tucker, W. *The Science and Politics of Racial Research.* Urbana, IL: University of Illinois Press, 1994.

Weinberg, M. *Racism in the United States: A Comprehensive Classified Bibliography.* New York: Greenwood, 1990.

Sharon Cronin
Seattle Coordinator

Chapter 2

◼ Roots of Resistance

Until the philosophy which holds one race superior
and another inferior is finally and permanently dis-
credited and abandoned . . . everywhere is war.

—Bob Marley, "War"

One day, as I observed a European American teacher present a lesson on the Civil War to a third grade class, the topic of slavery came up. An African American girl commented, "I heard that when Africans were on boats coming to America, if someone got sick they were thrown overboard. Why would somebody throw someone off a boat because he was sick?"

If you were the teacher in this situation, how would you respond? Would you feel nervous? Put on the spot? Would you feel adequately prepared to answer her question? In another class, I observed an African American boy with a dark-brown complexion telling an African American girl with a light-brown complexion that "white girls don't know anything." The African American teacher sent him out of the room and talked with him later. How would you have interpreted the boy's comment? Where do you think it came from? What would you have said to the children if you were the teacher?

Many teachers are not well-prepared to deal effectively with incidents of racism and issues of cultural identity such as these; nor do they typically know effective ways to nurture children in building a strong sense of identity while providing tools for them to identify and challenge racism and other forms of prejudice.

To be truly prepared to address the questions children raise, to give them guidance, and to provide leadership in forming just and healthy learning communities, teachers must have a solid understanding of our own personal histories, as well as the history of our culture, which means we need to

- know who we are;
- understand and be able to explain how racism and other forms of oppression work to keep people down; and
- know our own history of resistance and the history of other communities.

Only by personal reflection and listening to the experiences of others can we begin to understand the history of prejudice and the resistance against it, which will allow us, as teachers and parents, to create an environment in which children are able to realize their fullest potential and humanity.

CRAB and Personal and Social Histories of Resistance

Relating stories about our experiences with oppression was one of the first activities the CRAB groups used to get to know one another. We used a variety of questions to uncover memories and begin discussions:

- What are some of your first memories about racism? (This question can also be used to uncover other kinds of oppression. For example, what are some of your first memories about sexism, classism, or homophobia?)
- What was going on?
- How did you feel?
- How did the adults respond?
- What was your first experience with empowerment?
- How did it come about?
- What sorts of models and mentors did you have?

Sometimes, we initiated discussions by sharing an object, story, or ritual from our family's culture that supports our work in culturally relevant anti-bias education. For example, a photo album of several generations of strong women and a homemade quilt that has been passed down through several generations were shared. Also shared were the stories of celebration, resistance, and courage in the rituals of Hanukkah and Passover. One participant told the story about her father, a minister, who stood up against racism in the face of opposition from the rest of his white community.

Telling and sharing stories accomplished two purposes. First, CRAB participants were able to get to know one another on a deep level. For people of color, sharing stories was especially validating because it may have been the first time they shared their story with others. Second, sharing stories provided practice in what Brazilian educator and organizer Paulo Freire calls "reading the world" or "conscientization" (becoming aware or conscious of one's own environment and the power relationships present). Telling stories allowed us to remember and revisit our own experience and, in the process, to identify the power relationships we had experienced in various situations. Once the power dynamics involved in each story and their relationship to the power dynamics in the community and the society were clear, we began to discuss how we would like them to be and to formulate the strategies that would be needed for transforming them.

Many people of color shared stories of ways their parents and others supported them through their early encounters with racism. These stories were both painful and empowering, ranging from very violent overt racial attacks to subtle encounters. For some people, the racist incident they had experienced was so subtle they hadn't realized they had been a victim of discrimination until much later. Yet, within each of these stories were the roots of resistance to the oppression.

We Each Have Our Own Story of Resistance

I see culturally relevant anti-bias work with children and families as coming from a long tradition of people resisting oppression in the Americas, beginning with the first acts of European economic, racial, and cultural oppression. As coordinator of the Seattle CRAB group, I found a major source of strength in my knowledge of the history of people's resistance and the skills I have learned from elders and community organizers that made me the person that I am. I can't continue to do this work without continuing to learn from, acknowledge, and honor those ancestors who brought us forward to this point.

One of my early recollections of beginning to understand and resist racism was when I went to play with a European American girl at her house. We had played together the whole day. Her Auntie had not taken a good look at me when I came in, so it wasn't until the afternoon when my mother came to pick me up that Auntie realized I was not entirely of European heritage. Her whole presence changed. She became very cold and stern. She did not speak a word to my mother. She just glared at us. Then she took an old rag and began methodically wiping everything that I had just played with or touched.

I remember sensing that something about me had really changed in her mind. I knew it was unhealthy and illogical, since I was still the same little girl. I also noticed that my mother was not fazed or surprised. Mom just looked at the woman and gathered me up with my things and we left. We talked about the experience in the car on the way home. I don't remember if my mother used the word *racism* to define my experience, but she did give me words to name what had happened.

Since then I have had many other experiences with racism. But the way my mother guided me through that early incident helped me to be prepared, to understand what was going on, and to figure out my options for responding. More important, my mother's guidance taught me that I must not allow that incident to define my self-concept. Nor should I internalize the negative or racist messages of others or society. In other words, I learned not to buy into the philosophy "which holds one race superior and another inferior" as described in Bob Marley's song.

Later in my life, other family members—aunts and uncles, my grandfather—offered continued guidance and support. I realize now that this support helped us to defend ourselves against the psychological and physical attacks of racism, as well as to construct strong, positive, viable self-concepts and identities within our own culture.

Cirecie Olatunji, the New Orleans CRAB project coordinator, has often pointed out that parents of color can spend so much of their time responding and reacting to racial and economic forms of oppression that they rarely address positive cultural development of their children. At the same time, parents of color also need to reflect on the role of internalized oppression, or hatred of one's own ethnic or cultural group, in their children's development and how it affects the child's interactions with others from the same ethnic group. This reflection involves reclaiming and continuously examining and re-creating how a cultural group wants to be as a people. A group's cultural identity, and therefore a child's developing cultural identity, is centered around the events, interactions, and activities of a community, as well as the daily interactions of family members at home, school, and in the community.

Cirecie shared an example of how internalized oppression played out in her daughter's life at a predominantly African American public school. Lighter-skinned children were calling her "African Girl," because of her last name and her darker complexion. This incident shows how the other children had internalized the racist standards of the society around them (in this case, the belief that it's better to have lighter skin and to shed connections with one's African heritage). In response, Cirecie continuously reinforced how beautiful her daughter was and talked with her about the origin of these attitudes and comments.

I have listened to many parents of color describe in detail the strategies they use to support their children in developing positive self-esteem and what Samuel Betances defines as "rejecting rejection." These strategies often include parents talking with their children about the kinds of experiences that they might encounter. One parent said, "I tell them all people have different views, and racism is against people of different cultural backgrounds learning how to integrate their own work together. I stress that they should be proud of who they are. I tell them that people may laugh at who they are, the way they wear their hair, but it doesn't make them any less." Some parents have the children practice what they might say or do in different situations. As children of color get older and move out into the larger community, especially the young men, their parents become more concerned for their safety. The message that parents give to their children changes. Because of the high incidence of police violence against young men of color, parents of color often coach them as they get older about how to deal with the police.

Parents and family members have been teaching children to "reject rejection" throughout the past 400 or so years of our country's history, beginning with the first Native Americans and Africans who escaped from slavery and formed their own communities, resisted and fought back, or kept their culture alive in ways hidden from the plantation owners. However, in my experience, not all parents of children of color have had the benefit of the community's collective knowledge of how to resist oppression. And some parents may believe it is better to shield their young children as long as possible by not teaching them about racism until they are older, or at least until they actually encounter a racist incident. Still others have a good sense of how to support children of color in rejecting rejection, but they have not provided their children with the tools they need to construct a positive cultural identity and sense of self, and yet others may focus on cultural identity but not teach the historic roots and institutional dynamics of racism.

European American children have parallel needs to children of color for learning to resist oppressive messages and to construct a sense of self that is not based on a philosophy of superiority. I have met European American parents who have done an excellent job of negotiating this balance, largely because they had spent time examining their own biases related to race and other forms of oppression. These parents are committed to providing ways for their children to learn about their European American cultural identity without internalizing a sense of superiority. They help their children understand the meanings of fairness and justice. They introduce and expose their children to stories about European Americans who fought against oppression throughout history. They create alliances with communities of color and actively work on a better world for all children.

Many other European American parents want their children to resist learning prejudice, but they either do not realize the direct role

they must play or in fact do not know what to do. A large number of these parents do not see themselves as having a clear cultural identity, and therefore they do not intentionally consider how to nurture their children's positive sense of cultural identity separate from the racial identity of being white. And, sadly, many European American parents continue to teach their children, both directly and indirectly, that being white is superior.

It seems so natural now to discuss this notion of the cultural root-lessness of many white people in our Seattle group. However, it was a new concept to many. In all three CRAB groups, we found that many European Americans did not give much thought to their own culture, because they were so immersed in it and found validation everyday for their physical appearance, communication and interaction styles, and language. Some didn't feel that they had a culture. As a group, we had to process the fact that European American parents had a choice about whether or not to use culturally relevant anti-bias parenting strategies and work to "undo" racial oppression. The privilege that being white grants in our society ensures that white children will not suffer economically or socially if they don't understand the dynamics of institutional racism. For people of color, because of the way society responds to our physical appearance, communication style, and cultural practices, having to deal regularly, often on a daily basis, with the issues of racism and Eurocentrism was pretty much guaranteed. Therefore, parents of color are forced to deal with the issue of racism in their parenting to ensure the best possible future for their children.

Many of our European American CRAB participants said that Peggy McIntosh's article "Unpacking the Knapsack of White Privilege" (see resources) was very helpful in their developing an understanding of how white privilege functions in ways that are often invisible to white people. I know their development of this understanding was a significant part of the cross-cultural community building and development of trust in our Seattle group. I quickly notice and appreciate European Americans who recognize the privileges and advantages that they accrue through being white. They are definitely better able to be allies and friends with people of color, and this recognition is truly the basis for developing solidarity. I remember how effective it was (and how supported I felt) when one of our European American members brought up a plan in one of our meetings to address the needs of children who speak a home language other than English. By then, I was tired of always being the one to bring up this issue. I really felt the collaboration.

Resistance is Important to Children's Development

Racism is children's enemy, and undoing it is the responsibility of both people of color and European Americans. Racism attacks and damages children of color by attempting to rob them of their cultural center. It leaves deep personal scars on an individual's sense of self-worth and creates barriers to accessing housing, health care, education, and employment. At the same time, racism undermines the humanity of white children, teaching them a false sense of self based on the supposed superiority of a particular skin color and giving them permission to misuse, dislike, and fear others for no other reason than the other's different identity.

Not giving all children a sense of who they are and who their people have been cuts them off from incredible sources of strength, knowledge, and guidance. As Sharon Henry, co-coordinator of the Minneapolis/St. Paul CRAB project, has pointed out, if children don't know who they are, they cannot be wholly human. As adults, if we can't speak with our own voices and in our own way, then we can't stay intact or whole, and we can't effectively resist oppression. In other words, the importance of knowing who we are to our development, to our ability to meet our own needs, and to resist oppression puts culture at the center of our work with children.

There are parallel issues for European American children from poor and working class families—especially if the way they speak English is different from Standard English. The negative messages that these children receive about their background, family, home life, and history can cut to the core of their self-esteem and inspire a tremendous sense of shame. I remember a European American training participant who said she didn't really have a culture. I asked her where her parents and grandparents were from. She first said Texas, and then said, laughing, "and before that they were those hillbilly people you see on TV from rural mountain areas." Others laughed, but I didn't. I said quite seriously, "There will be European American children in your programs and classrooms who will share this cultural background, and they will need you all to model pride in this important heritage." I think I received the worst evaluation feedback ever on that training session, and it made me think about how much work we have to do to "undo" classism and other oppressions, as well as racism, in our work with children. All children need to feel pride in where they come from and find it as a source of strength and courage.

This is the challenge we face as parents and educators: How do we balance the struggle between supporting children in understanding how racism and other forms of oppression work on the institutional level and also support their natural development of a sense of internal beauty and pride in who they are? If children don't have that deep sense of self-worth and clarity in their cultural identities, it makes it harder to resist racism directed at themselves or others. If they don't have a sense of how institutional racism has worked historically and in its present forms, they will not have sufficient tools for developing within and building their own cultural centers.

To help children develop a strong sense of self and a positive cultural identity, educators need to teach children how to reject rejection, as well as how to stay in their "right minds." This concept came out of coordinators' discussion of Alice Walker's book *The Color Purple*. At one point, the character Celie becomes agitated and psychologically uncomfortable. She realizes that she has wronged another woman in her family by her advice to her stepson that he should beat his wife to make her "behave." Celie recognizes that it was her envy of her daughter-in-law's strength and defiance that caused her to give this advice. She also comes to realize that she won't be able to get back to her "right mind" until she apologizes to her daughter-in-law and attempts to right the wrong her advice has caused. Those of us in the discussion of this episode took being in your "right mind" to mean staying in your own center (culturally or otherwise) and not being confused or pulled away from it by constant attacks of racism or other forms of oppression. In order to accomplish this, it is essential to lay the groundwork of knowing where one's cultural center is—not just basing one's ethnic identity on responding to, resisting, and reacting to racism, but also doing the difficult work of reconstructing, reclaiming, and re-creating our collective and personal cultural identities.

If parents and educators want to help our children reject rejection and stay in their "right minds," then we must also reconstruct our cultural identities and strengthen our ability to resist racism (and other forms of oppression). Cirecie Olatunji introduced the CRAB leadership group to the concept of reclaiming our humanity through "corrective development." This means uncovering and ridding ourselves of the beliefs and feelings that keep our minds and hearts chained to false ideas about who we are and the behaviors that keep us participating in our own or others' oppression. Through the process of corrective development, we all become more fully human and can better nurture our children. As CRAB group members discovered and developed our individual senses of our cultural centers and began to see ourselves as cultural beings committed to undoing racism and other oppressions, we found that a deep sense of cultural identity was a source of great strength for CRAB members.

A member of our Seattle group shared that this concept was similar to the concept in Latino culture of "el niño bien educado" (the well-educated child). It does not just refer to academic or book knowledge; more importantly, it refers to learning how to be a caring, contributing, respectful, ethical person. This is the commitment each member of the CRAB groups took on throughout our time of working together. The commitment to this kind of personal growth, which made us capable of being effective in struggling against racism, was essential to the success of the project.

Exploring our cultural identities and what it means to gain a sense of wholeness by staying in our "right mind," another important piece of our growth in the CRAB groups was addressed with questions such as these:

- When you think of your cultural center (or your "right mind") what images do you see? What does it feel like?
- Draw a picture or make a collage of your cultural center.
- When are you most in your "right mind"?
- How do you know when you start to slip out of your center? Make a list of the places or times in your day when this happens.
- What can you do to regain your center?

Early Childhood Programs as a Place of Resistance

The struggle against oppressions in education is about creating conditions in which children can stay in their "right minds." Child care providers and teachers of all grade levels are major players in creating a genuinely safe and supportive educational environment where children's interests are served. In such a classroom, the children do not have to leave half or more of themselves outside the door when they come in. In such a classroom, the lines between home, community, and school are flexible and interactive. In this type of environment, children can learn about the whole world and its variety of cultures and lifestyles without sacrificing their sense of who they are and where they come from, their cultural center.

In my own growing up, a handful of school counselors, a few teachers, and a "minority liaison" in my high school made a critical difference for me. Interestingly enough, the woman who was my minority liaison twenty years ago, Coleen Amojuela, joined our Seattle CRAB group. I was honored with her presence, which brings the development of my cultural identity and capacity to resist oppression full circle. I remember a time in high school, however, when I was just frozen when the teacher was presenting incorrect information about people of color. It was that day in the curriculum when, finally, African American history would be covered. It took less than one class session. There were just a couple of things to say about "slaves," as if there was no history prior to that time period for people of African descent. And no mention was ever made of the maroons who escaped slavery and established independent communities or of any people, black or white, who resisted the institution of slavery. I couldn't say anything. I just painfully sat there with my face on fire and the palms of my hands clammy.

In response to this incident, the leaders in the community organized a meeting with the school board and helped the students of color get together and prepare what we wanted to say about our experiences. I will never forget that day. I can't remember a thing that I said standing up there before the school board, but I do remember getting up the strength to talk to what appeared to be one large unit of European American men in suits. The support of our mentors and other adults in our communities was essential in enabling us to speak out, and we were better prepared to talk in other situations because of this experience. After that, I went to my history and social studies classes with my own sources and was never quiet again.

Many teachers are not prepared for the task of supporting children when they are learning to resist biases and reject rejection. Some teachers of color are in a sort of limbo—with prompting they can recollect roots of resistance in their lives, in incidents or ongoing patterns of racism and the rich solutions that they observed on the part of the adults around them, although this knowledge base is buried. As a result they haven't had the opportunity to apply the knowledge hiding within their memories to their work with children. When most early childhood teachers went through professional preparation, they were trained in "developmentally appropriate practices" and given the message that there is a universal pattern of development for all children, and therefore a way of teaching that best supports the development of all children. In reality, however, the practices that were promoted as best practices for all children were really based on the culture and value systems of the people who created them—the European American middle class. For example, in the original discussions of developmentally appropriate practice, there was a bias toward encouraging children's independence and individualism—a European American value that is not shared by all other cultural groups. Due to this kind of bias, teachers of color were pushed into letting go of what we knew about raising children of color (if we wanted to pass our training courses). We were pushed away from our cultural center and prevented from staying in our "right minds" in relation to caring for and teaching children of color. Many educators of color have experienced tremendous stress trying to incorporate developmentally appropriate practices instead of what our common sense and the collective wisdom of our cultural communities said was best for our babies.

Because of this conflict, many teachers of color began to reexamine what early childhood education could be for children of color. The changes in educational programming that resulted from this work came to be called "culturally relevant education" or a "culture-centric approach" (for example, Afro-centric programs and bilingual/bicultural programs). Reexamining and re-creating culturally relevant programming for children is in itself an act of resistance. This work also is now beginning to influence the official position of the National Association for the Education of Young Children (NAEYC) on developmentally appropriate practices. The revised *Developmentally Appropriate Practice* published by NAEYC now clearly states that culture is a critical component of a child's development and must be thoughtfully included and respected in all that early childhood practitioners do.

This important first step sets up the next essential and long-term task of transforming early childhood practice not only with children, but also in teacher training and research. Defining what "cultural relevance" meant to members of the CRAB groups and how the concept would be applied in our work was a central part of our work. We spent time learning about and presenting our cultural backgrounds and family histories.

This fueled our discussions and projects at our respective places of work. We challenged each other to think about how these discussions and concepts applied in each of our work environments. Working to incorporate these concepts in early childhood education is also another step in the long history of resistance against the cultural oppression of racism.

The Eurocentric nature of early childhood education theory and practice works ultimately to the detriment of European American teachers also. They think they have been trained to understand the development of all children, but in actuality they only know about the development of one group—European Americans. Thus they are ill-prepared to work with children of color. Though European American teachers may have every intent of supporting all children's learning equally, they can often do harm through their ignorance of cultural norms for children of color. For example, teachers at one preschool were ignorant of the fact that in many cultures children are allowed to keep a pacifier or suck their thumbs until they stop voluntarily. They insisted that a three year old was too old to keep his pacifier, when it was perfectly normal and acceptable in his home culture. Seeking better preparation in culturally relevant early childhood care and education is an act of resistance against cultural racism. Doing so enables European American teachers to fully carry out their professional commitment to nurturing all children. Our CRAB groups were a nurturing and safe haven for participants to discuss some of their ideas for developing culturally relevant curriculum.

Key Lessons in the History of Resistance

I vividly remember when during a workshop on racism I realized for the first time, and with great clarity, the historic economic roots of modern racism. The presentation was on the indigenous people's early struggles against racism in the "New World" (or the Americas) and the infamous fifteenth-century debate between Bartolome de las Casas and Gaines de Sepulveda regarding whether indigenous people had souls.

In the first fifty years that people from Spain and other European countries were present in the Americas, they had decimated the indigenous populations on many of the islands and mainland communities by means of murder, new diseases, and capture for the slave trade. Slavery was not a part of Europe's economic system at that time, but its reinstitution was to prove a powerful means of reviving a failing economic system. In order to justify the reinstitution of slavery in the face of pressure from Europeans who did not accept its barbarism, it was necessary to invent lies, first about the indigenous people in the Americas, and later about African people.

Bartolome de las Casas was a Franciscan friar working as a missionary in the Americas in the 1550s. He was appalled by the treatment of indigenous people in the Americas and returned to Europe to advocate on their behalf. Gaines de Sepulveda was an excellent debater and theologian who was asked to defend the practices of the emerging merchant class in the New World. He claimed that the inhuman treatment was justified because Native Americans did not have souls. The debate went on for some fifteen years. Finally, Bartolome de las Casas won the debate, and laws were passed to limit the cruel treatment of indigenous people of the Americas. For example, they could no longer be forced to dive for pearls for extensive periods of time or be overworked in the sugar cane industry. However, Gaines de Sepulveda had successfully planted the seeds for a philosophy of racial superiority. And when a similar question was raised about Africans and their treatment in the Americas, the outcome was not as favorable. De las Casas himself initially supported the use of Africans as slaves, but by the end of his life he recanted that position. In his life he carried out acts both of racism and of resistance—a dynamic in the lives of many people to this day.

The most powerful historic lesson in resistance for me has been that, from the beginning, indigenous and African peoples resisted the psychological and physical oppression of racism. Some managed to escape slavery and establish independent communities. Spanish, French, and British colonizers used the term *maroon* to refer to Africans who escaped from slavery to set up their own communities. The word *maroon* is derived from the Spanish word *cimarron,* which referred to cattle and other animals who ran away from their domestic sites to live in the wild.

The escapees called their acts of resistance *maroonage,* claiming the name for themselves.

Creating maroon communities, whether physically and psychologically, is part of both African American and Latino histories. Some of these communities still exist today in the Caribbean and South America. There have also been numerous examples of both physical and psychological maroonage all over the Americas, though they are not included in U.S. history books. One aspect of these efforts especially relevant to us today is the continuous struggle by people of color in the Americas to preserve their languages. For example, very few people are aware that communities in the Americas still speak variations of their native African Yoruba and Akan languages, thus retaining their language for more than 200 years.

Asa Hilliard recently introduced the concept of maroonage to the educational community. He calls on us to keep alive the sense of a community-in-struggle that evolved from the early efforts of African Americans to reject notions of European racial superiority. One way we can continue that tradition is by teaching children of color to resist attacks on their personal worth, dignity, and competence by providing them with an education deeply grounded in their own cultural orientations, heritage, and experiences.

It is important for both people of color and European Americans to know the proud history of resistance of people of color. This information profoundly challenges the myth that people of color were or are passive victims of oppression. Knowing the history of resistance has the power to shift our frames of reference so we can see the truth. As people of color, we have done a good job of surviving conditions even worse than now. Yet we have to reflect back to see what got us through those other times, the strengths we relied on, the effective and ineffective strategies, the lessons for us today.

Resistance to racism also has its own history in European American communities. This, too, is important for everyone to know. In his well-documented 1993 book, *Anti-Racism in U.S. History,* Aptheker describes innumerable acts of opposition to racisim by European Americans ranging from individual acts to participation in organized movements for change with people of color.

Our history is present. We just need to ask questions like the following, which we used in the CRAB groups:

- What has been the history of resistance in your community?
- How could you find out?
- What sorts of historic documents might be available in your community's libraries or archives?
- Which elders might be able to tell you stories about how they resisted in the past?
- Are there labor or civil rights leaders who could add information?

Get together with a few other people—perhaps enlisting the help of a high-school history class. Conduct interviews, dig through personal and public records. The information is there—we need to uncover it and give it new life.

Knowledge of the history of resistance to racism can also be used as a model for learning about the history of resistance to other forms of oppression such as sexism, homophobia, classism, ableism, religious persecution, and ageism. These different forms of oppression are often interrelated and have shared histories. We all need to know about the innumerable alliances among various cultural groups and between people of color and white resistance. We all need to know what worked and what disrupted those alliances. These are important lessons for our current work.

We Raise Children

The concept of the community collectively raising children is at the core of CRAB work. Learning to reject rejection, resist racism, and reconstruct cultural identities is a collective process. So, too, is uncovering the stories of resistance in the communities where we live and work. In my community, some of us have set up a bimonthly Saturday group for children of African descent and their parents from throughout the diaspora. We learn songs in English, Spanish, and Yoruba as well as dances from our rich heritages, and parents take turns reading or telling stories. We use the dances, stories, and discussions to teach the children about themselves and about the history of peoples' resistance. The children have added activities of their own, including an open-mike session where they practice being an audience and performing in front of the group.

Connecting our current efforts to our communities' history of resisting injustice enables us to place our work in a larger context, build upon what is there, and learn from our elders about the strategies and tools that work to help us in that resistance. That history also inspires us to construct the next steps of the journey so that others may take up where we leave off.

Resources

Aptheker, Herbert. *Anti-Racism in U.S. History.* Westport, CT: Praeger, 1993.

McIntosh, Peggy. "White Privilege: Unpacking the Invisible Knapsack." In *Peace and Freedom.* July/August 1989.

Walker, Alice. *The Color Purple.* San Diego, CA: Harcourt, 1982.

Sharon Henry
Minneapolis/St. Paul Co-Coordinator

Chapter 3

The CRAB Group Approach: Personal Reflections

There is no task more challenging, no job more demanding, and no investment more promising than nurturing the healthy development of our children. The future of our society rests on the shoulders of those who want to live in healthy communities where the developmental needs of children are primary. In such communities the vision of the future includes people willing, prepared, and committed to caring for their own and secure in the fact that people who are different from them—whether by current economic status, economic class of origin, or culture—are partners with them in seeing this vision come true.

The Early Childhood Education System is Failing Children/Families of Color

As an African American woman and through my work as an administrator for a community-based child care resource and referral organization, I have come to believe that the current early childhood education system is non-affirming for people of color and incompatible with who we are as educators, parents, children, and members of a community. Like most other disciplines specific to children and families, early childhood education is unable and unprepared to address the continuing and, in some cases, growing assaults on our children and communities. How do we actively deal with the reality that children are increasingly experiencing domestic violence and the loss of extended families because of depressed economic conditions that force families to move away from relatives? How do we actively address the fact that children are increasingly witnessing violence and degradation against their neighbors and family members by police officers and gangs?

I have seen how training approaches, advocacy strategies, or simply functioning within early childhood organizational structures require many of us to unlearn what we know as people of color and members of our communities. For example, in infant/toddler training there is no room for our ways of holding our babies, or for our beliefs about where and in what they should sleep. Putting babies to sleep in an isolated room separate from the everyday activity of other children (common and accepted practice in most early childhood programs) is not culturally appropriate when children are used to being put to sleep in an environment that is active with human voices, music, and the hubbub of living activities, as happens in many African American families. There is no room for our own terms that indicate stages of growth, such as "knee baby" for toddler and "nursed baby" for a child who is breast-feeding. Instead, people of color are coerced into accepting, as though we bring no knowledge of our own, a body of knowledge, theory, and practices that are European-centered and, in many cases, irrelevant or even harmful to the real needs of our children. For example, dominant child development theory teaches that anxiety around strangers is a developmental stage; however, this is not necessarily a developmental hallmark in families or cultures where many adults nurture children and infants move comfortably from one caring adult to another. Another example is the significant difference in the emphasis placed on individual autonomy. European American culture and, consequently, child development theory, emphasize the importance of the early development of individualism, which is in contrast to the greater emphasis placed on the value of interdependence in the cultures of many ethnic groups of color.

When an early childhood program bases its ways of working with children on one culture's primary values, it places children from other cultural contexts at risk for inappropriate handling and for misinterpretation of children's needs, behavior, and abilities.

The early childhood profession affirms European American culture as the rule to which other cultural ways are the exception. Early childhood education practice is much more likely to build on the experience and perspectives of European American teachers, parents, and children than of others. Child development theory is built primarily from observations and studies of European American children, although it is often presented as universal. Moreover, because European Americans are members of the politically dominant culture, they are encouraged to perceive themselves as individuals rather than as members of a community, as cultureless products of the great melting pot, and, ultimately, as superior. Therefore, it is difficult for European American early childhood practitioners to recognize or appreciate the fundamental role of children's home culture in their development or the ways in which the values of European American culture are imposed in defining early childhood standards and "best practice."

Each day I see our children, our families, and our communities suffer in a system that reproduces and maintains inequities and perpetuates a European-centered status quo that elevates European American culture to the status of universal and denies the importance of other groups' cultures in the healthy development of children. I see how we are faced with the painful reality that racism and other oppressions marginalize children's sense of self and require adults to relate to each other defensively and with hostility.

So the question must be asked: Why are we continuing to use care and education approaches with children and families that are ineffective at best and damaging at worst? Why are we ignoring the voices of the communities? Who should be our partners in reshaping this system so it is responsive to the real needs of all children? And what will it require of each of us to accomplish this goal? Participation in the CRAB project required us to ask, struggle with, and begin to answer these questions.

The CRAB Project as One Strategy for Change

My attraction to the CRAB project was based on my belief that I must try any and all avenues I could find to improve conditions for people of color. I first learned about the CRAB project from Stacey York, who was already involved in CRAB and came to my office to tell me about it. Though I had already begun my own work in creating culturally affirming child care environments, I considered the questions that involvement in the project presented: If I don't participate, what will they do? Could this be an opportunity for me to find resources and opportunities for people of color? Finally, I felt I must step into the unknown because it might result in something good for people of color.

Although these questions imply that I believed I had some type of power to pass on large-scale benefits to people of color or that people of color would be beneficiaries or recipients of something important, I must admit to you right now that my perceived power was simply that—perceived. The Creator has humbled me, and I now understand that the journey was about me.

Please let me offer you some of the insights and lessons I gained in my CRAB journey. I was blessed to travel this journey in the safe company of my sisters—Cirecie Olatunji, Sharon Cronin, and Stacey York, and the project director, Louise Derman-Sparks. I have come to understand that my work is in building coalitions, in challenging myself and others to develop a deeper understanding of the impact of racism and other kinds of oppression on children, and in working to heal the scars these have left on us as adults. Please remember that, as it was for me, your most important learning will happen with your own partners in this journey.

The CRAB Approach and Community Organizing

Community organizing is fundamentally about reclaiming our humanity and recognizing that we don't live in isolation from each other. One of the best examples in recent U.S. history is the Civil Rights movement. It was made clear from the beginning that this movement was not about "Negroes"—it was about everyone's humanity. What I am talking about

here is moving from the feeling of being paralyzed to dialoguing with others to create positive change.

The CRAB approach is a community-organizing strategy that concentrates on prioritizing and improving the care and education of our children by mobilizing parents, classroom aides, classroom teachers, church mothers, pastors, family physicians, and anyone else interested to act on behalf of children. No one person can do this work. Besides, if I tried to act alone, I would become worn out and beaten down. It would also be arrogant for me to assume that any one person can either determine a community's agenda or facilitate the profound change that is needed.

During a National Public Radio Press Club broadcast about his experience teaching music to young people, musician Wynton Marsalis commented, "This is the thing that is so difficult many times to convince our younger students of—that it is important for you to view yourself in the context of everyone else." Marsalis then described an exercise in which he has young musicians play a segment of a piece and then describes the role or notes of another person in the ensemble who plays a different instrument. Inevitably the students have focused on their own part and are not aware of the other musician's role. Through this exercise Marsalis actually teaches a lesson about being human, about the importance of knowing yourself and your responsibility in the context of being part of the whole. I was blown away by how this lesson so eloquently captures the essence of why I do my work in early childhood education and what it means to reconstruct human will in the best interests of our children.

Thinking of community organizing as a strategy that can both move people to action and enable them to reclaim their humanity helps me maintain a balance between the cultural and political aspects of my work. In other words, I do not want to overemphasize the cultural aspect yet never take political action. Conversely, I do not want to jump to political action without also attending to the cultural aspect.

I often see frontline practitioners and advocates for caregivers and children getting stuck in the dream and rhetoric of what cultural, spiritual, and emotional health and well-being will look like for our children,

families, and communities without concretely creating and implementing strategies for change. This results in much talk but little action. Or sometimes I see people immediately leaping to political strategizing without taking the time to discuss and imagine a vision of what we want, what needs to change, and how our multifaceted identities (culture, class, gender, and so forth) affect how we work to get there. This leads to devising strategies that are based on the intent to create change, which inevitably end up maintaining or even enhancing the status quo. For example, getting more training resources for caregivers without first consulting with communities of color about what they want for their children can result in teachers better trained to carry out European-centered early childhood practices.

Understanding the process of "reclaiming our humanity" has been incredibly exhilarating for me. I have consciously focused on my own development and gained greater clarity about my role in my community and my responsibility to my people. By being confronted with this new context, this different way of thinking about the impact of racism on my own community and struggling through that, I've become clearer in my roles as parent, aunt, sister, coworker; a stronger ally; and a person committed to promoting the health and well-being of all people. In the past I thought only of very concrete examples of white privilege and its effects on African American people—sharecropping, lynching, separate toilets, and so on. Now white privilege seems more complex, and I wonder, what is the real effect of racism? How have we really been damaged? I have had to come to terms with the real impact of racism on my community—that it is this loss of humanity—and that this is just as relevant for white people as it is for people of color.

This lesson came to me not only from our discussions in the CRAB groups specifically, but from the process of trying to figure out why the CRAB groups weren't meeting the needs of people of color. I learned because I had to reach out to my community to look at healing for my people, and in that way, this lesson was a byproduct of the CRAB group.

"Moving the Center": The Challenge of Multiethnic, Multicultural Coalitions

Working in a multiethnic, multicultural coalition means facing hard issues and struggling to "move the center." That means uncovering and facing the power dynamics of racism and then changing them into new ways of being with each other. More than once I questioned my role as an African American woman in the CRAB project. As I reflect on my three years in the Minneapolis/St. Paul group, what happened in that group has become clearer. In the first year of the project, we spent most of our time on the role, responsibility, and agenda of the whites in the group. We focused on making changes within the early childhood system, where several participants had some leverage. By so doing, we nurtured the journey of the whites at the expense of the people of color (although that was not our conscious intent). It wasn't until one evening in one of the intensives that I was moved to challenge myself and reach out for help.

We had come to the end of our day and we had shifted into social groups. I sat on the floor with one group and began to listen to the conversation. An African American woman who has a considerable reputation within the local early childhood community was talking about a shooting that had taken place in our community and expressing her terror for her own children as well as her general pain, disgust, fear, and anger at the incident. When I heard her words, I immediately felt sickened by the conversation. I began to feel anger directed at her. Why was she saying these things in the presence of these white women? I immediately felt she was "exposing" our business.

I was also aware that a tornado of anger, pain, and fear was going on inside my body and my mind—and the feelings were not just about her. I shared my feelings and puzzlement with one of the other African American women in the group. She confirmed that my feelings were not crazy and that she had also felt the need to talk about ourselves with one another in a closed environment.

I understand now that my feelings were about our need as African American women to begin our own journey separate from the white women in the group. The priority of our discussions and our work needed to be ourselves, our needs, and the needs of our children, families, and our community. We needed to "move the center."

When I opened up these issues to the rest of the women of color in the Minneapolis/St. Paul CRAB group, I heard from almost all members about their concerns over their roles in the project and its real value to their people. For example, some of the women related their supervisors' expectations of them to train staff at their workplaces as payback for allowing them to participate in the project. This posed a conflict for them because they had joined the CRAB group to give to their people, to their own cultural communities (however they defined community), and training a primarily white staff was not their idea of how best to do this. Moreover, the Minneapolis/St. Paul CRAB group's primary focus on changing early childhood systems and training early childhood practitioners (the majority of whom are white) resulted in the women of color in the group feeling that the white women in the CRAB project, rather than themselves, were prioritizing how women of color would best meet the needs of their own people.

How to "move the center" within the context of our CRAB group became a priority for the women of color. As a result, some of the African American women organized a Saturday group that met in our community for about ten Saturdays. We also continued to participate in the CRAB group. We asked a sister from our community whom we all respected to facilitate this group and help us focus on our feelings and process together what we were experiencing. We became clear that the CRAB experience was valuable to us only if we redirected our energy and put our children, our community, and ourselves at the center of the agenda. By doing this, the women of color took the necessary time to think about and discuss the manifestations and impact of racism on their people and on themselves, with the intent of figuring out ways to improve conditions for generations to come. This resulted in greater focus on working within our own communities, rather than primarily focusing on training European Americans in existing programs and early childhood organizations.

As this experience demonstrates, whether it is cross-cultural or culturally specific, a CRAB group can provide a supportive community coalition that challenges each of us to

- check out our beliefs;
- question the origins of those beliefs when necessary;
- embrace the origins of some beliefs as a source of strength; and
- understand and put into practice the importance of culture in any effort to improve conditions for our children within the early childhood education system or heal our communities.

If we are to reclaim our humanity, it is essential that we affirm our ways of being as Latino, African American, Native American, Asian American, and European American people.

For an example of how culture must be considered as a central part of rethinking early childhood education, consider the statement, "I don't see color when I look at children"—one I frequently hear from people in the early childhood field. While this may be an expression of acceptance and love for the individual making the comment, many others experience a rush of discomfort and rage upon hearing it. From my perspective, the "color-blind" belief diminishes me (regardless of the intent of the speaker) and is not good for children of any culture. I am a cultural being, and the color-blind perspective denies that to me because it invariably reflects the belief that "we are all the same." My color is relevant to my experience as an African American woman in a racist society that uses skin color as a determinant of who is and who isn't entitled to power and privilege. Moreover, my community knows it is vital to our children's health to resist put-downs based on skin color. That is why you may hear people refer to people's skin color as chocolate brown, dark brown, light brown. The color of our skin is not something to be ignored, but something to be celebrated by paying attention to and describing it. A color-blind position denies this reality.

I want to be seen, understood, and treated fairly for all that I am—that is what lets me have my full humanity. So if people think that claiming they don't see color when they look at children is the way to nurture healthy children, then I want them to understand the consequences of that belief for me and my children, as well as the implications for our ability to communicate. Collaboratively examining the deeper reality underlying such a statement leads to insights about the nature of European-centered privilege and its ability to make it possible for people to think that a color-blind perspective eliminates the problem of racial prejudice. It also makes it possible to understand that maintaining cultural integrity, in spite of the many serious obstacles to doing so, is essential to survival.

As we move on through our journey toward healing from the assaults of racism and unlearning the lie of white superiority, we also understand more deeply the relevance of culture as a force for reclaiming our humanity in our work with children, adults, and communities.

Eliminating Internalized Oppression and Internalized Privilege

One critical piece of reclaiming our humanity is uncovering, understanding, and eliminating internalized oppression and internalized privilege. If we do this correctly, we create an environment where we can learn from and teach one another. In this environment, when one of us expresses a belief that is harmful to others, the ideas underlying it and the feelings it provokes in everyone present can be openly discussed and processed.

> *Internalized oppression is the acceptance by a member of an oppressed group of the biases of the dominating group, and consequent self-oppression.*

One of the lessons we learned in the CRAB group was that we needed to spend time discussing not only white privilege but its parallel for people of color. We used language like "internalized oppression" to name it, but I think it was too easy to just say that. It was easy for us to think of behaviors in our communities that reflected internalized

oppression, such as "black on black" crime, genocidal alcoholism, gangs, prejudice against members of our own community based on skin color, hair texture, and so on. We all could come up with these experiences and examples very easily, but we knew it was deeper and more complicated.

When some African American members of the CRAB group began to meet away from the group, we did not discuss internalized oppression. We never got to that discussion, and I think that was a mistake. However, as I look back on that now, I understand and appreciate the wisdom of the sister who nurtured us through our process. She forced us to see how our people never did and, to this day, do not "accept" the biases of the dominant group. Our resilience has been due to our resistance. Sharon Cronin says it so well, "I realize now that this support helped us to defend ourselves against the psychological and physical attacks of racism, as well as to construct strong, positive, viable self-concepts and identities within our own culture."

Still, we have not really learned to integrate the profound impact on people of color and white people of economic oppression, attempted cultural genocide (such as the experiences of boarding schools for Indian people, internment camps for Japanese American people during World War II, or the slavery and postslavery experience for African people and their descendants), or the "legitimizing" of racist ideology in the United States into our understanding of internalized oppression and internalized superiority.

Staying Connected to Our Primary Cultural Communities

As we found ourselves taking this incredible journey in the CRAB group, we were all challenged by the complexity of human relationships embodied in the group. Having connection to our primary cultural communities was critical to handing the many challenges effectively. The CRAB group and the coalitions we created among ourselves do not and should not replace strong connections to our own primary cultural communities.

In my opinion, the individuals in the CRAB group who did not have a connection to their cultural community (regardless of their cultural background) or felt alienated from it demanded an inordinate amount of time and attention from the group. They wanted the CRAB group to meet their needs for identity and connection, which went beyond the purpose or ability of the group. While strong and supportive relationships evolved among the group members, the group was at heart a network of people from varying backgrounds working together on shared goals. The stronger a member's connection was to her primary community, the more she was able to contribute to the group, and the more she was able to grow without losing her cultural center. Conversely, the weaker the member's connection to her primary cultural community, the less she had to bring to the group, the more she expected from the group in terms of connection, and the easier it was for her to lose her cultural center.

A learning community such as the CRAB group can enable members to gain greater clarity and confidence about themselves, as it did for me, but it cannot do it all. If a person finds it a challenge to define her primary cultural community or is disconnected from or rejects her own people, the healthiest thing to do is to find ways to reconnect and expand her consciousness within her own community. Then each of us can come to the "multicultural table" ready to work in a multiethnic coalition.

Another key aspect of being connected to our own primary cultural communities is that it enables us to be clearer about our agenda. In some cases, we are already very clear about our agenda, based on our own and our community's lived experiences. Sometimes we understand what needs to be done on an emotional level, yet don't have the words to articulate these feelings. In these cases, it is important that we not give up on what we know intuitively. Listening to others and discussing issues within our community will give us the words and voice we want, which we can then bring to a learning community such as the CRAB group. Listen to the pain, the silence, the weakness, and the strength, even though at times it may be hard. This knowledge and passion fuel our work.

The CRAB strategy helps to create a wide community loop, or network, of people who are committed to redefining and modeling the principles, values, and behaviors we want our children and communities to take on. Within this loop, our children can move from one environment or segment of the community to another and be affirmed at every turn. As the loop grows, the area of affirmation and safety for our children grows as well. The CRAB approach is one way of expanding this network.

Members of this community loop see themselves as architects of change. We understand that we do not live in isolation from one another. The ability to heal ourselves and our communities comes from building relationships and identifying and pursuing strategies of change. We therefore continue to build networks that are diverse in culture, religion, occupation, income, neighborhood, gender, class, ability, and so forth. From these will grow communities that care for *all* of their own, communities that will provide safe shelter and responsible care and attention to generations to come from birth through death. These caring communities will serve as a moral, nurturing foundation for *all* of our children.

The CRAB strategy offers one way of organizing around the needs of the children in our communities. However, our implementation of CRAB strategy is not a blueprint to be followed without any adaptations or changes. Many kinds of community-organizing strategies have been used by disenfranchised communities for centuries (the Underground Railroad is one that immediately comes to my mind), and communities continue to create ways to resist oppressive institutions and build services that meet their children's needs. Don't be afraid to adapt our approach and experiment with other models to meet the needs of your particular community. Be willing to do your own thing, and let us know what you're doing so we can continue to learn from one another.

Stacey York
Minneapolis/St. Paul Co-Coordinator

Monthly Meetings and Training Retreats: An Opportunity To Struggle, Learn, and Grow Together

> In the struggle for justice, the only reward is the
> opportunity to be in the struggle. You can't expect
> that you're going to have it tomorrow. You just have
> to keep working on it.
>
> —Frederick Douglass

The CRAB project brought diverse groups of early childhood educators together. The project required a lot of us. It challenged us to claim responsibility for ourselves, increase our knowledge, and improve our communication skills. It placed us in a learning laboratory where we built and strengthened our cross-cultural relationship skills. It tested our commitment to the struggle for justice.

Through this experience we learned the importance of relationships. We structured the groups in ways we hoped would help people come together, build relationships, and agree to a common good. We asked participants to make a three-year commitment to the CRAB group. The CRAB groups used two formats for gathering, building relationships,

learning, struggling, and working toward change together. Two- to three-day training retreats and short monthly meetings were complementary ways of creating a learning laboratory. The retreats and monthly meetings allowed us to witness and experience firsthand the pain and contradictions of our society. The meetings were structured around meals to foster fellowship. We also used dyads and small group discussions to foster relationships.

On the one hand, each of us came to the group wanting to heal ourselves and our communities. We wanted to be with others who also cared passionately about the dehumanizing forces threatening our lives, who wanted to take action to heal our communities, and who wanted to increase their self-awareness and experience more authentic cross-cultural relationships. On the other hand, we stumbled over ourselves, our hurts, our betrayals, and our lack of information as we all struggled to work together. But again and again we kept coming back to the table, trying to make it work, deepening our understanding.

We also learned the importance of helping individuals develop skills and become more competent. Becoming more competent included working on ourselves so that we could become more effective in cross-cultural work. We were engaged in incredibly difficult, perhaps unprecedented work. We were trying to work together to fully understand the dynamics of racism, sexism, classism, ableism, heterosexism, anti-Semitism, ethnocentrism, and ageism. At the same time, the nature of oppression is to create barriers and stunt our development as human beings. Whether in the oppressor or oppressed role, CRAB members found it difficult to establish and maintain authentic relationships across racial and cultural lines. Each of us had to face the ways in which we had been shaped by racism and ethnocentrism. Those who were able to do this brought a greater degree of integrity to their work.

Through this process, we learned that our individual behavior affected the relationships and the work of the group. For example, growing up white in America, I had internalized a false sense of superiority. As a result, I tended to speak for people of color, finish their sentences, or have the last word in a group discussion. Once I became

aware of this, I needed to work on my behavior and change it so that I was more effective in cross-cultural relationships. Each of us, at one point or another, moved the group forward or slowed the group's growth by our behavior.

Planning Retreats and Meetings

"Okay everyone, get out your calendars. We need to select the dates for the next retreat before Louise leaves. The weekend of the seventh? Nope. How about the fourteenth? Well, what about the twenty-first? Anybody

Considerations for Planning Monthly Meetings
- Will there be food at each meeting? If so, will it be a potluck or will the project provide snacks?
- Will participants be able to bring their children? Will on-site child care or reimbursement for child care expenses be provided?
- Whose language will be used?
- Will we begin or end the monthly meeting with a ritual? If so, whose ritual?
- How will the group deal with time issues? Will meetings start on time, or when everyone has arrived?
- How will the details of the monthly meeting and retreats be communicated to participants?
- How will we choose the site for the meeting? How will you take into account various participants' different levels of comfort and familiarity with different meeting sites and times?
- Who will facilitate the meetings? Who will organize them? Who will decide who facilitates or organizes the meetings? How will you decide?
- How much meeting time should be taken up with organizational issues, and how much time should be devoted to "content"? Who decides? How is the decision made?

for the twenty-eighth? Hmmm. Let's go at this another way. Raise your hand if you *can't* come on the seventh."

Finding dates when everyone could get together was impossible. Finding dates when *almost* everyone could get together for a monthly meeting, let alone a retreat, was really difficult. Everyone was busy. Each of us had families, demanding jobs, and commitments to numerous projects and organizations. Consequently, a lot of thought and energy went into setting up, planning, and facilitating the retreats and monthly meetings. Initially, the local coordinators were responsible for organizing the sessions, often consulting Project Director Louise Derman-Sparks and the coordinators about what to do next. As time passed, participants began to take responsibility for planning and organizing the retreats and meetings.

Through the retreats and monthly meetings, each project site developed its own unique character. One group generated a list of monthly meeting topics on the last day of the first training retreat. This move allowed a volunteer committee to plan the work of the monthly meetings far in advance. Meetings took place at different group members' homes or work sites. The host sometimes played a specific teaching role in the meeting.

In another group, the local coordinators met between meetings to process and evaluate the previous meeting and plan the next. Originally, meetings rotated back and forth between participants' work sites around the city. Eventually, the group found a "home" at an American Indian church.

Two of the groups held their meetings during the day or late afternoons, while another met in the evening. All groups met monthly, with meetings lasting three to four hours.

At all three project sites, the coordinators tried to be inclusive of participants' cultural styles in planning and facilitating. At the beginning,

Participants' Comments on CRAB Group Membership:

"It was great to be a part of a group of people who cared about the same things that I do and who are making a difference little by little."

"Our retreats and group meetings are a chance to share things that I would have difficulty sharing elsewhere, even in my own family."

"I know that I can call up any of the people from the CRAB group and say 'I need help.'"

when we didn't know much about the participants or their cultural styles or needs, these attempts were as simple as planning to meet in a noninstitutional setting (in Minneapolis, the first meeting was held in someone's home), making sure there would be lots of food, and planning to spend some time in racially specific groups.

Retreats

Each CRAB group began the journey through a four-day training retreat. After that, each group met monthly and held shorter one- or two-day retreats twice a year. The retreats were a rare and precious opportunity to meet without distractions and to build our group.

The retreats provided each of us with an opportunity to search deep within ourselves. Here we could finally voice our ideas about our work and the things we were sensing in a relationship or in ourselves. For example, a participant might say to the group, "There's something about my training that's not working and I haven't had time to think it through. I haven't had anybody to talk to who thinks like me or who is doing this work." So the training retreats were an opportunity to reflect with others and bring new thoughts into full consciousness, to push ourselves to figure out how our individual and group identities were shaping our role in this work. For example, just because I'm a woman doesn't mean I automatically understand sexism, and just because I'm white doesn't mean I understand the role whites play in racism. We needed time to put our experiences into an analytical framework.

For some participants, going to the retreat meant taking a big emotional risk and facing their fears. Those of us who were introverts, private, or cautious about intimacy sometimes felt overstimulated or exposed at retreats. Even for extroverts, maintaining a high level of interpersonal interaction for two or three days can be challenging. Also, we were dealing with such intensely emotional issues and all of us were in some senses trying to be on our best behavior around the issues and one another. If we were going to make a mistake and offend people, it would likely be at a retreat, where deeper exploration of the issues was possible. Some people were reluctant to take that risk and so avoided the retreats, came late, or left early. Some faced their fears head on and transcended them.

It was important for the groups to pay attention to the emotional stress inherent in the retreats. Was it useful for the groups' work to place people in emotionally vulnerable positions? At what point did a retreat or intensive become invasive and damaging to people? Site coordinators needed to assess the participants' comfort level with everything, from the site and the meeting's format to the food, with the idea in mind of minimizing participants' stress levels. For example, the Minneapolis group held many of its retreats at retreat centers an hour out of town, requiring participants to sleep overnight. This style of retreat seemed to be more beneficial to European Americans. The Seattle group did not go away to hold its retreats, enabling participants to go home each night. This seemed to work better for people of color, enabling them to be home with their families at night. The New Orleans group had overnights but stayed in the city. These three ways of handling the retreats provided different levels of comfort for different participants, and in some ways the differences correlated with cultural differences. Thus in the attempt to minimize stress at the retreats and make them more manageable for participants, it was necessary to consider cultural differences.

The retreats sometimes became really intense. Sometimes we would spend twelve straight hours in deep discussions on the first day. By the second day, we were worn out, and by the last day, we were no longer functioning and couldn't even hold a large group discussion. As a result, we learned that we needed lots of participants' input so that the agenda was more balanced between individual and group times, work and play, learning and entertainment, and sitting still and moving our bodies. We had to remember to feed our hearts, bodies, and souls, as well as our minds.

Monthly Meetings

Monthly meetings built upon the momentum created in the retreats, challenging and supporting group members to keep growing, to keep moving on in their journeys. Many training models use retreats as their main vehicle but do not keep participants together over time. In the CRAB project, monthly meetings were an essential component for providing the

structure to build strong, ongoing relationships among group members and to support their personal growth and activities at their work sites, their training of others, and their advocacy efforts within early childhood and other community organizations.

All group members wanted the monthly meetings to provide a combination of support, encouragement, and networking, as well as knowledge, information, and skill-building. However, individual members' ideas about the appropriate *balance* among these various areas differed widely, so planning how to meet every member's needs was complicated and demanding.

Many times, the monthly meetings were primarily business meetings, where we responded to requests for training, planned how to participate in community events, discussed current events like the Rodney King riots in Los Angeles, helped people who had specific concerns, and had presentations on specific topics.

As participants began to take action against forms of oppression in their communities, they looked to the monthly meetings to sustain them emotionally as well as to get feedback and new ideas. The monthly meetings were also a vehicle through which local coordinators monitored the progress and outreach activities of the group.

Again and again, no matter what the meeting topic, participants struggled to get their needs met within the group. From the local coordinator's perspective, it often seemed

Participants had widely varying expectations of the monthly meetings, as shown by this selection of comments from one Minneapolis/St. Paul meeting:

"I think we need to get better at networking within this group and integrate networking into the work of the group."

"The group hasn't helped people to do training. We should take advantage of some of the thinking on different approaches to training. We should bring in someone from outside the group and get specific training."

"The group should be a place to get feedback and support on issues."

"I think we need to work on internalized oppression."

"I want specific training so that I feel comfortable talking with friends and neighbors. I'm afraid to take the plunge."

"I want to figure out how to work effectively with people in our own communities."

that no members ever got enough of what they were looking for at any one meeting. If the session focused on sharing, the folks who wanted new information interpreted the meeting as poorly planned, unorganized, or not useful. If we spent the session focusing on new information, some participants would complain that we never had enough time for sharing or that the topic wasn't relevant to their needs. If we spent time examining and processing our group's dynamics, people who wanted to focus on their outreach work felt too much time had been spent on internal group issues. Regardless of the scheduled topic, heartfelt immediate issues sometimes had to take precedence, at least for part of the meeting. All of us were experiencing isolation and alienation in our CRAB work on the job, and some were facing retaliation from supervisors for participating in the project. There were many needs to be met in such a short amount of time.

Over time, however, we managed to meet the various needs of the group members. We also learned what worked better at retreats rather than at the monthly meetings. For example, exploring a topic in depth was best done at retreats.

I also learned that it is easy for the groups to get sidetracked at monthly meetings. European Americans as a group tried time and time again to switch the focus from the issues raised by people of color (which tended to be more personal or intimate, such as dealing with internalized oppression) to statewide initiatives. It seemed as though it felt too complex or too emotionally tender to European Americans to pay attention to these more immediate issues. Instead, in general, they found it more interesting and more relevant to talk about systemic issues, like how the state provided resource and referral services to people of color, or how we were going to train all child care providers in the state to be culturally competent. We needed to monitor the monthly meetings for this kind of Eurocentrism by asking ourselves questions like, Whose community is this work important for? Whose children are being served by this project? Whose voices are being heard or silenced in this meeting? Whose personal or professional agenda is being furthered here?

As expected, given the complexity of the groups' needs, individual participants' feelings about the meetings ranged over a continuum. The

differences didn't seem to break down along class or race lines but seemed to reflect the participants' different learning styles and individual needs. Many members regularly commented that they found the monthly meetings helpful and would really feel "lost" and left out if they missed a meeting. Other participants reported dreading the monthly meetings. However, even those who had ambivalent feelings about the struggle involved in making the group meetings work still felt they benefited from them. For example, one member of the New Orleans group said she'd always remember about the monthly meeting the day of the meeting. She'd try to find any and every possible excuse to avoid going, but then drag herself there. During the course of the meeting something would always happen—someone would make a personal breakthrough or something magical would be said—and all of a sudden she felt refreshed and nourished. By the end of the meeting, she'd say she was glad that she came.

Building a Shared Knowledge Base:
The Training Content and Process

There is so much to know in order to effectively work for change in our communities. For example, we all need to know about social oppression, resistance, culture, and identity development. We need to take time to increase our understanding and consciousness of key topics and current issues. In this way, the monthly meetings and retreats were training sessions to help all of us strengthen our knowledge and skills.

Telling Our Stories

Through the project, we learned how important it was to begin our journeys together by sharing personal identity stories. Telling our stories helped us uncover and celebrate our shared humanity. This was critical because we started with the agenda of dealing directly with racism, and that created a huge divide between participants. The difference between the experience of white people and people of color is so great that it's easy to get stuck in shame, guilt, and anger. Sharing personal identity stories formed the winding trail back to one another again across that divide.

> **Questions for Self-Reflection to Help Groups Discover Common Ground:**
> - What are the values and principles that we share?
> - What do we want for our children and families?
> - What are the dangers to our children?
> - How do I participate in what happens to children in my community?
> - What community strengths can support us in our work?

We spent the first retreat having participants tell their stories. Stories provided a natural way of bringing up sensitive issues without forcing them on participants. Beginning with stories gave the facilitators the information to plan meetings that were pertinent to the participants' needs. The stories showed us which issues were of immediate importance to groups members, and they gave us an idea of the group members' understanding of these issues. In addition, they helped us plan how much time to spend in dyads or small groups and large groups, and how much time to spend in racially separate or racially mixed groups.

Building Our Knowledge Base

The retreats and monthly meetings provided a time for us to learn together and build a shared knowledge base for our work. For example, we needed to take time in the training retreats and monthly meetings to educate ourselves about social oppression, resistance, identity development, and cultural development. Part of what the group did involved learning, analyzing, and strategizing about these topics and others.

The local coordinators carefully observed and listened to the participants at each meeting. After each meeting, the coordinators spent several hours analyzing what had happened and then checked in with the director of the project for another perspective on the meeting and the possible next steps for the group.

For the coordinators, it was like planning emergent curriculum with children—careful observation of the group process and then determining and trying to provide the resources needed to further the group's discussion. In this way, the meetings' themes emerged from the group participants and their relationships to one another and from events specific to our community. Whatever the topic, it was essential to bring the discussion back to the children and our particular communities.

Supporting Different Learning Styles

Once a topic or pressing issue had been identified, local coordinators needed to figure out how to structure the training retreat or monthly meeting where it would be brought up for discussion. This step was always challenging because of members' different learning styles and the need to balance process and product, reflection and action. It was difficult to meet the needs of multiple learning styles in a two- to four-hour monthly meeting. It was a bit easier to do so during the retreats, which were much longer.

To deal with the diverse needs and learning styles, we included a variety of teaching methods supported by current theories of adult development. All of the local coordinators had some previous experience in education, even in those cases where it wasn't their primary field of expertise. We all respected the need to touch the whole person—mind, heart, and soul—and we wanted participants to be active learners, fully engaged in the process. We also believed that each participant came

Some Topics Covered in Monthly Meetings:
Cultural Identity ◆ Cross-Cultural Communication ◆ Anti-Semitism ◆ Developmentally Appropriate Practice ◆ Racism ◆ Culturally Relevant Early Childhood Programs ◆ Ageism ◆ Stages of Adult Identity Development ◆ Adult Education Methods ◆ Sexism ◆ Anti-bias Curriculum ◆ Internalized Oppression ◆ Culturally Specific Parenting ◆ Heterosexism ◆ Parent Empowerment and Education ◆ White Privilege ◆ Policy Development ◆ Social Systems ◆ Community Organizing ◆ Being a Leader ◆ Advocacy Work in Organizations ◆ Ongoing Analysis of Local Needs of Children and Families ◆ Ongoing Analysis of the Early Childhood Community ◆ Bilingual/Bicultural Early Childhood Programs

to the table with knowledge and wisdom, and that effective social action and personal empowerment came from reflection, analysis, and strategizing with others.

Issues Changing Over Time

The CRAB project wasn't like a one-time workshop in which topics such as culture or racism are explored and then dropped. The combination of retreats and monthly meetings helped keep the content in the forefront of each participant's mind. The ongoing nature of the project also helped

Training Methods Used in the CRAB Groups:

dyads	brainstorming and webbing
triads	journaling
cross-cultural small groups	field experience
culturally specific small groups	visualization
large group discussion	processing group dynamics
simulation	lectures
panel discussion	rituals
racially specific small groups	debriefing
reading/reviewing literature	audiovisual presentations
role-playing	

people grow intellectually and develop critical thinking and greater self-awareness around issues of oppression. As the groups developed over time, the topics that emerged began to change. Still, while each site covered topics generated specifically by its members, there was a great deal of similarity among the sites regarding the topics chosen to discuss as well as the sequence in which they were examined.

Early on, some group members questioned, even challenged, the project's focus on racism as the central oppression for us to explore. Others challenged another underlying premise of the project—that we

had to look at other major forms of oppression and how they all interacted with each other. This struggle revealed the complex interactions of the different types of oppression. For example, in all of the CRAB groups, especially at the beginning, the coordinators noticed that the topic of other types of oppression (classism, ableism, heterosexism) was typically raised by white participants who experienced them, when the group was trying to address issues about racism. During the first training retreats, whenever the issue of racism and the group's focus on racism came up, a white participant would bring up heterosexism, ableism, or another oppression, and insist that the group address that issue first. This was especially true when the white person involved was the only representative of a particular group—such as the only lesbian, or the only person with a disability. Being the only representative increased individuals' sense of isolation around the issue and also their desperation that their issue be addressed.

The coordinators were clear that it was necessary for us to address all types of oppression. At the same time, it was also clear to the coordinators that these participants were acting out of white privilege. Their privilege as white people allowed them to assume that they had the right to take "air time," to deflect the group's conversation from the subject of racism, to make the group engage in the struggle around which oppresion was most important, should be addressed first, or should get the most attention. Creating this kind of power struggle in racially mixed groups is a typical pattern of behavior for European Americans, arising out of our privilege as white people in a racist society. It was confusing for everyone because these participants were speaking legitimately from the position of the target of one of the other "isms," but they were doing so in a way that grew from their white privilege and, ultimately, was racist.

It was a huge challenge for the coordinators to figure out how to manage this complexity in the groups's interactions. In almost every case, it was very difficult to call participants on this kind of acting out of white privilege. The denial and resistance of these white people was very strong, and for a number of reasons. No one wants to see herself as act-

ing out of white privilege or being racist, particularly when most participants held the value of being anti-racist. Many of the white people were struggling with confusion about their own identities. White people are trained not to see white privilege, which in *itself* is about white privilege and racism. And members who were the only representative of a particular group (for example, the only lesbian, the only person with a disability, the only working class woman) were isolated in that respect, which made it very difficult for them to trust that the group would attend to their concerns. It also added to their resistance to being challenged about white privilege.

Through the experience of dealing with this dynamic within the groups, we learned that it was important to begin with participants' stories, to allow people to air their own experiences with oppression and feel heard by the group. It was also essential to address the issue of white privilege directly, which meant dealing with racism up front.

By the second half of the first year, core group dynamic tensions surfaced, which became key learning experiences. In New Orleans, only the European American members of the group showed up for the retreat being held at this time. The local coordinator, Cirecie Olatunji, knew that there were various reasons for the absences of some of the people of color in the group. She also suspected that unspoken tensions among the European American members were turning off the rest of the participants of color. She decided to use the retreat to process this tension with the European Americans. She also asked the project director to observe the discussion and the dynamics of the group without participating.

The ensuing discussion among the European American participants exposed the level of competition among them, which reflects one of the effects of racism on white people. Two of the European American participants had more experience with anti-racism work, were more politically active, and had more organizing experience. As a result, they saw themselves as further along in anti-racism work and interacted with the other European Americans with a kind of self-righteousness. This is a common dynamic among European Americans—the urge to be the "good white person" leads us to want to separate ourselves from other white people, not to be seen as "one of them." It is so abhorrent to us

to think of ourselves as racist that we want to pull away from the white political identity. The less-experienced European American members of the New Orleans CRAB group felt intimidated by these two women and were afraid of being judged. They responded by silencing themselves. The same urge to be "good white people" and the same abhorrence of being racist led them, as it often does with people who are less experienced, to withdraw from the process for fear of making mistakes and being cast as the "racist white person." The dynamic ignores what we really know—that white people are all racist by virtue of being raised in a racist society. Nonetheless, we all have crucial insights into dismantling the system, even though some of us have been working on anti-racist issues for a longer time.

At the retreat where this issue was brought into the open in the New Orleans CRAB group, Cirecie began the discussion by asking the participants to talk about what was happening for them in the group and how they felt about how the group was working. When the competition and subtle put-downs that had been going on came out in the open, there was some resentment on the part of the two more experienced women. However, one of them was willing to hear what people were saying and reflect on her behavior. She was able to engage in a much more personal examination of what was happening, and she understood the process and how she had participated. In addition, it was clear to everyone that there were two parts to the dynamic. The more experienced women had definitely been behaving in ways that separated them from the other European Americans and conveyed their own assumed superiority (for example, by putting themselves outside the group in the way they talked about how "whites do X" and "whites do Y" and lecturing the rest of the group from a position of more assumed knowledge). On the other hand, the less experienced white women had silenced themselves and had given the more experienced women the power to make judgments about them. As a result of this discussion, the whole group was able to understand the dynamic of the competition between white people for the role of the "good white" as one of the effects of racism on white people, and see how it had kept the group from doing the work it had come together to do.

About a year into the project, each of the CRAB groups did a "webbing" exercise to identify all of the activities that each group member was involved in as a result of participating in the project. Many people came into the exercise feeling intimidated, hesitant, and unsure that they were living up to their end of the bargain, which was to get training and share it with others. As each person talked about what she was doing, the facilitator wrote down the main points on a web diagram. As people shared the ways in which they were bringing the work of the CRAB group to their families, work sites, neighbors, and communities, a huge, intricate, detailed diagram emerged. People were bringing CRAB work into advocacy, parent education, caregiving, teaching, administration, organizational change, teacher education, networking, community organizing, public policy, and interpersonal relationships. At that point in the project, the participants were not sure they were doing very much individually. But, clearly, as shown by the web exercise, everyone was doing something, and together we had this web of activity. People began to feel excited and stronger. They sat up with smiles on their faces, leaned forward eagerly as the energy in the room increased. People talked about how seeing the whole picture gave them the energy and courage to do more.

In the Minneapolis/St. Paul CRAB group, both the people of color and the people who were not yet involved in training were especially strengthened by the activity. Sharing their experiences had revealed that a very important segment of their CRAB work was interpersonal, rather than organizational or occupational. People were talking about the issues that were coming up in CRAB group meetings to their family members, neighbors, and friends. Naming these conversations as CRAB work and including them on the web helped all of us realize that this was a legitimate outreach activity, every bit as important and valuable as conducting a workshop. This retreat was a high point for our group.

The web exercise was also helpful in moving people into further action. When members heard about one another's experiences, they began to say things like, "Hmmm, maybe I will try doing that" and "Would you be willing to do that with me? Because I don't think I could do it by myself."

Tools for Being an Effective Local Coordinator

The local coordinator role was very challenging and complex. Prior to the project, we were unable to fully anticipate all of the dimensions of the local coordinator's role. As we reflect back on the experience, we understand better all of the skills and tools a local coordinator needs, which has helped us recognize the extent to which the coordinator's role was not only challenging but also nearly impossible. Here's a list of the qualities we found indispensable:

- *Humor*: Be able to laugh at yourself and with others. Humor is often the best tool to break the tension that can accompany this work.
- *Insight*: Be able to read social situations and interpersonal dynamics and be sensitive to the tension, comfort level, and emotional state of each participant.
- *Negotiation*: A combination of mediation and problem-solving skills is needed to make sure everyone's voice is heard and that all participants feel represented.
- *Objective Observation*: Be able to stand back and see the whole picture while watching out for each person in the group.
- *Assessment and Evaluation*: Observe and assess each participant's growth and development, as well as the development of the group.
- *Organization:* Locate an office out of which to operate the group. Set up a budget, telephone service, and procedures for communicating with participants and taking training requests. Organize monthly meetings and plan retreats.
- *Delegation*: Be able to delegate tasks and responsibilities to group members by beginning with small tasks and then gradually increasing group members' responsibilities in maintaining the group.
- *Planning*: Be able to develop short- and long-range planning for the group.
- *Time Management*: Manage the meeting agendas and keep track of time. Help the group make decisions based on the limited time and an often overambitious agenda.

- *Group Historian*: Remind the group of previous discussions and actions. Summarize and recap meetings and agendas. Extract themes and principles from group discussions.
- *Keeper of the Stories*: Know and pass on the community history and stories of the cultural communities. Allow and encourage everyone's vision to be shared.
- *Shifting the Center*: Look at the group and figure out how to avoid falling into the default mode that keeps European Americans at the center. Monitor the languages used, the translation equipment, the agendas being served, the needs being met, and the communication and interaction styles of the group.
- *Play and Celebration*: Plan opportunities for the group to share meals, sing, relax, and entertain one another.

Each of the coordinators brought some, but by no means all, of these skills to our work. We all learned new skills and strengthened those we already had through our experiences facilitating and coordinating the CRAB groups and by talking with and getting help from each other.

Cirecie tells a funny story that captures the labor involved in preparing for a monthly meeting. The day of the meeting she'd go to Sam's Club and buy snacks. She'd carefully pick the foods and beverages, thinking to herself that so-and-so doesn't eat this and so-and-so likes this. Then she'd load up all of the stuff in the trunk of her car along with all of the project materials, which included cardboard boxes of forms, handouts from past meetings, articles, and resource books. Now, Cirecie always dressed for her monthly meetings. So in skirt, stockings, and heels, she'd carry this stuff down the stairs to her car, out of her car and up the stairs to the meeting. She knew she'd be carrying it back down the stairs to her car after the meeting, and then from her car up the stairs to her hall closet where it would be stored until next month. At the

> meeting, she'd reach the top of the stairs with her hands full and all out of breath. The participants would be sitting there waiting and would greet her, "How ya doing?" She'd respond tartly, "I'd be better if you'd go down and get some of the stuff out of my car!"

Personal Reflections of a Reluctant Site Coordinator

Eleanor Roosevelt once said, "You gain strength, courage and confidence by every experience in which you really stop to look fear in the face.... You must do the thing you think you cannot do." When Louise Derman-Sparks first approached me about the CRAB project, I was interested in the position of evaluator (which was originally part of the grant) and knew I didn't want to be one of the local coordinators. I was afraid it would be too much work, too much emotional pressure, and too much time in the spotlight. And even though I'm an experienced trainer and facilitator, I'm not masterful at either. I figured I'd make lots of mistakes and have to deal with all sorts of criticism and difficult situations. I thought, "No, that's too big of a risk for me to take. Somebody else can be in the hot seat."

As is often the case, the grant was funded, but not fully, and the evaluator position was greatly restricted. If I wanted to be involved in the organization and development of the project, I'd need to be the local coordinator. I knew that any time you try to bring a diverse group of people together there's going to be struggle, and I ended up putting myself right in the thick of things.

I found that the monthly meetings just about did me in. They meant witnessing firsthand the pain and contradictions of our society. Each of us came to the meetings wanting to heal ourselves and our communities. But living in a society that is so segregated and out of balance makes it difficult to heal. I'd ask myself, "How can I expect to be able to come together with others to heal our communities when I myself need healing?" Time and time again, I stumbled over myself, and we stumbled over ourselves as we struggled to come together. That process was painful and demoralizing for me.

As an introverted person, I find groups and meetings difficult even when I'm not at center stage and responsible for so much. I'd awake the day of the meeting with a knot in my stomach that lingered until after the meeting was over. I'd try to imagine what each person was going to say and how I might respond to the conflicts that were sure to arise. Prior to the meeting, I'd load up on caffeine and sugar, trying to get an energy boost that would get me through the three- to four-hour session. Of course that was the worst thing I could have done, because it would leave me with a headache and feeling totally spent.

While all of us found the task of facilitating the monthly meetings very challenging, others didn't find it as hard as I did. Because I was the only local coordinator who was European American, I was on the spot in a different way than the other coordinators. Because one of the effects of racism on white people is such a tremendous level of competition to be the "good white person," from the first meeting my leadership was under constant challenge from other powerful European Americans. This wasn't true in the same way for the other site coordinators, who were all women of color.

I've never put so much time and effort in processing one meeting and planning the next. I'd often think that I'd never given so much and gotten so little back. It helped a lot that I shared the responsibility for coordinating our site with Sharon Henry. We would meet for hours rehashing, interpreting, and analyzing what had taken place at the previous meeting. Based on our shared understanding, we would determine where we would go next with the group. But rarely did our carefully conceptualized meetings turn out as we predicted. Because of this, I found the ongoing meetings very discouraging and draining.

On the other hand, I loved the retreats. Perhaps it's because I'm an introvert and the retreats gave me an opportunity to have long conversations with small groups of folks. I also loved sitting back and watching participants interact with one another. And I loved how we could delve deeply into issues. We had some of the most intense two- to three-hour large group conversations that I've ever experienced. The retreats were both exhilarating and draining. I wouldn't want to give them up for anything.

Now you might be thinking, "Why on earth would anyone want to do something that sounds so difficult?" I'm not trying to be discouraging. It's just that this work can be very hard. There are very few models for successfully facilitating multicultural groups that are attempting to deal with multiple issues of oppression. And it's not just that there are so few models; it's that the work itself touches issues that are very close to who we are and how we want to see ourselves. There isn't general consensus in our society that these are even important things to think or talk about. In many ways, the cultural divides between people who are separated by oppression are so wide that we don't even have common understandings or language to talk about the issues. At the same time, there's a kind of societal denial that we're different at all, or that our differences are important, while there are also huge penalties for difference. It took every bit of skill I had to try to manage all of these factors in the CRAB group meetings. It pushed me to grow in ways I never thought I could. Despite the painful struggle at times, all the groups stayed together throughout the project, and we all kept coming back to the table— including me.

The message here is that we have to be willing to live with the pain and tension, and we have to be committed to one another even though we're not perfect and make mistakes. This work helps me reclaim my cultural identity and heal from white privilege. It gives me integrity and affirms life. I'm grateful for having the opportunity to struggle with an incredible group of people.

> Fall down seven times get up eight.
> —Buddhist Quote

Cirecie Olatunji
New Orleans Coordinator

Chapter 5

Toward a Model of Cross-Cultural Group Process and Development

The CRAB group is an important laboratory for building bicultural and cross-cultural competence. The process provides both the context for group members' development of cross-cultural skills, and the content of the work necessary to develop them. As the coordinator of the New Orleans CRAB group, I gained key insights into the development of cross-cultural competence. This chapter describes an emerging model of identity development for a multiethnic anti-bias group, based on my experience with the New Orleans CRAB group.

Learning Goals for CRAB Participants

1. To facilitate the development of a healthy personal and group identity.
2. To encourage and promote healthy cross-cultural social interactions.
3. To develop critical thinking around the issues of bias.
4. To encourage taking social action against bias enacted against ourselves or others.

To create the learning goals we used the four goals of the anti-bias curriculum approach for children (see chapter 1) and translated them to

meet the needs of adults. As I and the other CRAB group coordinators worked with early childhood educators around the country, we found that many educators were jumping over the first goal. They were really excited about emphasizing healthy social interaction and reducing bias about race, gender, ability, age, class, and sexual orientation, but they were not sure about what it meant to foster children's development of a healthy cultural group identity and how doing so helps to create healthy social interactions and reduce bias. This is not surprising. Our society is so race and color conscious that it is difficult to see culture. Since few of us have received training in this area for ourselves, how could we possibly know how to support the healthy development of cultural identity in the children and families with whom we work?

A core part of my work as a CRAB group facilitator was to model how achieving the first goal facilitates success at achieving all of the other goals and to engage the group in this process. Developing a healthy personal and group identity, the first goal, facilitates cross-cultural interactions. The third and fourth goals flow easily out of the first in that they involve personal and group empowerment. Once individuals know who they are and can think for themselves, then they can do for themselves and others. The CRAB group process allowed us to develop a sense of personal and group identity. As we grew together, we took risks to share our successes and failures.

In one CRAB meeting, a teacher shared her uncertainties and resistance about her work to raise children's awareness of bias in her preschool classroom. She told us that she had been using reading time to "shift lenses" with the children to encourage them to imagine different viewpoints in the story. As the children caught on to this critical thinking activity, they moved beyond the teacher's comfort zone. What appeared normal to the children felt frightening to the teacher. The CRAB group members encouraged her to trust her intuition, trust the children, and trust the process. She responded that it felt like she was "sliding into an abyss." The group encouraged the teacher to be led by the children—to slide into the abyss. She did. Today that teacher shares her story with others as an example of how the group process in the

classroom can lead toward the development of personal and group identity for both the children and the adults.

Phases in Building Cross-Cultural Group Dynamics

Whether in the CRAB groups, in the classroom or in staff development, we found that the group process developed in three predictable and essential phases: establishing ground rules, testing the ground rules, and transforming the ground rules.

Establishing the Ground Rules

In its initial phase, the group established ground rules for behaviors it believed would enable the group to work together. However, these initial rules, although well-intentioned, tended to describe "politically correct" surface behaviors designed to keep the peace. They did not support behaviors that would open up and address the deep issues with which the groups had to grapple if both the individual members and the group as a whole were to grow. For example, in the New Orleans CRAB group, one of our initial ground rules was that everyone's ideas were to be treated without judgment, which in practice really meant that no one could ever question or struggle with anyone else's ideas.

In the early stage of group development, the New Orleans CRAB group members were idealistic about the future of the group. Members pictured themselves making sweeping changes in the early childhood community and in the lives of children. Individuals were focusing outward, thinking about what they could and would do to affect others. As time moved on, the group members began to focus their attention inward, reflecting on their own lives, their own experiences, and their own biases.

In this first phase the CRAB groups got stuck in the niceties of maintaining existing relationships. Many participants felt threatened by the possibility of rock-

> **Some New Orleans CRAB Group Rules:**
>
> Confidentiality
> Mutual Respect
> Creation of a Peace Zone
> Honesty
> Free of Biases

ing the boat by looking more deeply into their interactions. The members were not yet paying attention to aspects of the group environment or interactions that assaulted the culture of some of the members—for example, where meetings were held, the lack of child care, the organizational structure of the meeting, who did and didn't speak, whose agenda topics got attention, not allowing for and not listening to the silences, and so on. A significant event—usually a "blow-up"—was needed to move beyond this initial phase.

Testing the Ground Rules

In the middle phase, individual members started testing the group's initial ground rules. They may have been wondering "Is the group *really* a safe environment for individuals to share true feelings? Will I be put-down as biased or racist if my peers think I am saying the 'wrong' thing?" During this phase, CRAB group members often expressed that they felt confused, lost, and frustrated. Individual members of color backed off, saying, in effect, "No more, the price is too high, 'they' just don't understand!" (or, essentially, "This is too hard!") and individual white members backed off, saying, in effect, "I'll just stick to what I know best" (or, essentially, "This is too hard!"). A group may actually lose members at this point (which happened in all of the CRAB groups) or even dissolve. Groups may also attempt to hold their ground by reverting back to phase one "polite" behaviors, which is also a kind of dissolution of the group, because little growth and work can then be accomplished.

Transforming the Ground Rules

Transformation of group members' individual and group identity characterizes the final phase. Group members learn to understand and feel comfortable living with the complexities and inconsistencies of their own and the group's growth. Especially important is coming to accept in themselves and in the other group members the ongoing push/pull dynamic of moving toward awareness and personal growth and moving away from the group to avoid facing one's issues around bias. In this phase group members "stay at the table" when the going gets rough by

learning how to manage the internal conflict (living with oneself) as well as the external conflict (interactions among group members). The group takes on a new identity, one that reflects an interweaving of individual members into one unit.

By the end of the three-year project, CRAB members could laugh and joke with one another about their differing viewpoints and would often interject opposing opinions regarding CRAB practices when training as a team. I remember attending an NAEYC conference workshop led by a panel of CRAB members. They were able to articulately present a range of views on whether people who are not African American could conduct Kwanzaa ceremonies. Participants commented on how impressive it was to witness the CRAB model in action among the presenters.

Cross-Cultural Group Development: The Spiral Progression

Within the three phases of group development, a spiral progression captures the movement and growth of the interpersonal dynamics at work in the group. The points of the progression include the following:

1. Identifying the issues.

2. Establishing a safe environment.

3. Establishing and enforcing group norms that foster respect and empathy through honest and inclusive cross-cultural discussion.

4. Facilitating healthy conflict management.

5. Using the key points of resistance and tension as "teachable moments."

6. Supporting the development and testing of new, corrective, bias-free behaviors.

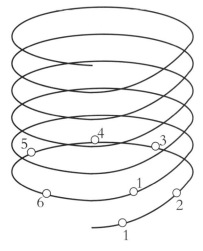

This process is not linear. The CRAB groups couldn't say, "We started here and eventually arrived there." Humans are complex beings and constantly changing, both as individuals and in relation to one another. So, in reality, collectively and individually we grow some and then need to loop back and work on an issue again, and then we grow some more and loop back, although usually not all the way back, and so forth. We constantly revisit all of the six points, in any order. It is a spiraling, dynamic, never-ending process that demands continual assessment of both the group's and individual members' growth and change. There is no final point, no end to be reached in becoming "anti-biased," either as a group or as individuals.

Point One: Identifying the Issues

The CRAB groups began here by identifying desired individual and group growth outcomes. As growth occurred, individual and group needs changed, so identifying the issues became an ongoing activity. We used a number of techniques to periodically uncover and identify our issues: dyad work, small group activities, individual and group journal writing, personal reflections on each meeting, and retreats. One exercise I adapted from the cross-cultural work of Paul Pedersen, *A Handbook for Developing Multicultural Awareness* involves a triad model in which a third person joins a dyad to observe and facilitate communication between the two active dyad partners. I also recorded these interactions on video for the whole group to analyze the nonverbal communication in the triads.

Point Two: Establishing a Safe Environment

In our first CRAB meeting in New Orleans, we wrote the most wonderful statements about what would enable us all to feel "safe" in the group. And it was safe until someone decided to test the limits of safety by disclosing one of her biases.

In a monthly meeting, a person of color decided to open up to the group and disclosed opinions on homosexuality and its relationship to community building in her particular cultural group. A person of European descent challenged her opinions and told her she had no right to be in the group if she had those attitudes. As the group

facilitator and an African American woman, I supported the person of color's right to place her opinions "on the table" for discussion in the group. Another participant of color supported the European American woman by stating that the facilitator had no right to say anything. Louise Derman-Sparks, the project director (who is of European descent) reestablished boundaries by reinforcing the facilitator's right to interject. The room fell silent and the meeting ended shortly thereafter.

During this incident, all of our carefully constructed rules went out the window. Out of the painful analysis of what had happened, we came to the important realization that the environment wasn't safe just because we said so. It was only going to be safe when we started working at it. Creating a safe environment is not simply an intellectual process of creating what we think are "politically correct" rules. It is a process that really begins when we don't rush to cover up or patch up a conflict but instead begin to collectively commit ourselves to create the safety. We have to feel safety in our hearts. That means tapping into our feelings, as well as our ideas, and being willing to deal with strong feelings. Moreover, the behaviors that constitute safety change as the individual members and the group as a whole develop.

Collectively committing ourselves to creating safety was a slow and arduous task that occurred over several months. What happened was a miracle. The more we learned about ourselves and one another, the more we respected the differences among us, and the more we trusted each other. We collectively established a safe environment for social change as well as personal growth. Some of the activities that we used to create the safe environment included the following:

- separating into two groups (whites and people of color) to discuss more sensitive topics that individuals were not willing to share across cultural/ethnic groups;
- going on retreat to have extended uninterrupted time to share our thoughts and feelings; and
- inviting guests into our group meetings who presented viewpoints that may have been present in the group, but had not heretofore been heard.

Point Three: Establishing and Enforcing Group Norms that Foster Respect and Empathy through Honest and Inclusive Cross-Cultural Discussion

New group norms of behavior emerged within the CRAB groups from our experiences with one another. We realized by trial and error that we needed to establish and enforce new expectations and rules as we came to understand their importance from our experiences and became willing to really commit to them. For example, after the individual in our group shared her opinions on homosexuality, our group was forced to realize the inadequacy of our initial ground rules. We had to face the fact that we were a microcosm of the larger society and as such invariably brought biases and subtle kinds of competitiveness into our interactions. Therefore, a new group norm emerged: facing these biases and competition, understanding them, and working at changing what we could while also caring for one another.

One of the hardest discussions in the New Orleans group was among the European American women. A subtle hierarchy had developed among them, with the politically active community organizers at the top and the early childhood practitioners at the bottom. These women were able to confront one another about the perceived judgments at a retreat when only European American participants came. Classroom teachers shared comments like, "I felt that if I talked about my failures in the classroom, you would say that I'm a racist." Or, "I disagree with some of your political arguments in the context of the CRAB approach, but I've been afraid of being labeled a political 'lightweight.'"

The community organizers were surprised to hear these statements and encouraged the members to share more. After the group of European American women was done processing and negotiating, each of them walked away with a more accurate and respectful perception of themselves and one another. As a result of this retreat, one of the community organizers was able to incorporate experiences, attitudes, and skills borrowed from the early childhood practitioners into her anti-oppression training. In the group at large, being honest and authentic became new norms that were quite different from the initial polite ground rule that required being

nonjudgmental with one another but didn't call on us to acknowledge the outstanding disagreements in the room.

Point Four: Facilitating Healthy Conflict Management

From my experiences facilitating the New Orleans CRAB group, I came to believe that conflict *management*, rather than the more traditional approach of conflict *resolution*, is essential to cross-cultural group development. This approach acknowledges that differences in perspective, tensions, and conflicts are real, inevitable, and growth producing. Moreover, conflicts occur within each of us as well as between us as we open up, rethink our experience and our opinions, and work on various identity, cross-cultural, and equity issues.

Conflict management brought needed fluidity to the CRAB experience. In the beginning, when we practiced conflict resolution, our meetings were characterized by pregnant pauses, deathly silences, and personal secrets about our biases. We were afraid of our differences and saw them as potential conflicts. We suppressed our passion about our ideas, which in turn prevented us from fully participating in the growth process. We made statements like, "We agree to disagree," but inside we felt that our voices could not be heard.

In the end, when we learned to practice conflict management, we felt happy about our differences and looked forward to passionate discussions with divergent viewpoints, because they became opportunities to expand our way of thinking and viewing the world. We learned to embrace the conflict as a point of discovery.

For example, dealing with resistance from colleagues and workshop participants was a recurring issue for us. CRAB group members' comments reflected their frustration and anxiety about what to do (for example, "Those teachers were so angry when I started talking about racism. *They* aren't ready to hear the truth about their biases"). To become clearer about why other people resist these issues, I challenged CRAB group members to consider these questions: Do these same issues cause resistance in you? When do you experience resistance? What are you feeling when you are turned off? Once we were able to explore

these questions, we were able to look at our own contribution to some-one else's resistance. We could honestly consider further questions: Was I being condescending in my delivery? Was I still uncomfortable about these issues? It is a natural, human response to define someone else as the Other and dismiss her, saying internally or aloud, "Damned if I know why she acts that way!" As a result of engaging in our own group process, we learned to truly appreciate an opposing opinion or ideology to the point where we reflected on whether or not we could accurately articulate what the Other was thinking.

Conflict management allowed group members to get in touch with and figure out how to manage their own anxieties about the process issues and content of the discussions. When we tapped into a topic that made one of us feel uncomfortable, we realized that it required us to do some self-analysis and self-assessment to really face ourselves in an honest way. We also recognized and applauded ourselves and one another for wanting to change and for staying at the table when the going got rough. Managing tensions and conflicts became a key part of both the process and content of CRAB training.

Point Five: Using the Key Points of Resistance and Tension as "Teachable Moments"

The technique of using the difficult places of inner and external resistance and conflict to deepen our cognitive understanding of the underlying issues is similar to early childhood practitioners' use of questions, comments, challenges, and dilemmas arising from children as "teachable moments" to build curriculum.

There are numerous opportunities for using this strategy. It is impossible to avoid making comments that reflect the oppressions in our society, even when participating in a multiethnic group devoted to growth in culturally relevant anti-bias education. All of us born or raised in the United States have been socialized into behaviors that reproduce oppression. People of color are taught to behave in ways that accept the oppression from the dominant group, and European Americans are taught to act out the privilege that whiteness bears in a color-conscious society. This socialization process is so subtle that we often do not know

when we are acting out these behaviors. Whenever a member of the group says something indicative of socialized privilege or internalized oppression, that can become a teachable moment. The objective is to explore it, work through it, and thus deepen the understanding of our own and others' key points of resistance.

However, adults often do not face and use such moments for growth as they arise. Typically, we either expend our energy on covering up the tensions or we get angry at others. Because these statements tap into other experiences of hurt, we often respond by wanting to shut down or shut people out. How we shut down has to do with our individual makeup. Some people put up a wall, say nothing, and are mentally gone for the rest of the meeting. Other people respond with anger and criticize or lash out at the person making the offensive statement. The important issue is not how any individual shuts down but knowing that we all have this tendency, which keeps us from using the power of our discomfort to deepen our understanding of oppression. Anxiety is a key component in change. I say to people, "If you haven't tapped into something that makes you uncomfortable and that requires you to do some self-analysis, to really face yourself, then there will be no change."

The group is wonderful because you know you can count on it, that you have this back-up. It does take struggle. There are going to be some bumps and tumbles. Once you allow time for that and keep processing you understand that it takes time, and challenge, and in some cases pain.... Also important is understanding that when the going gets hard you don't get to drop back into that old mode. You do get to work on your issues and know you will get better at what you are doing and that people will help you.

—New Orleans
CRAB participant

Yet facing feelings is not the end. As the four anti-bias goals for children remind us, we don't stop at developing empathy; we also go on to foster critical thinking. The goal at this point in the developmental progression of the group is to put our responses on the table and discuss them, to analyze them critically and come to new understandings about how we each respond to our key points of resistance. In brief, the teachable moment strategy means taking those key points of resistance from the heart to the head.

A man went into a bar and asked for a glass of red wine. He took a sip and threw it in the bartender's face. When asked why he did that, the man apologized, said he couldn't help himself, and asked for the name of a good therapist. Several years went by. One evening the bartender looked up and saw the same man at the bar. He asked the man how therapy turned out. The man said the therapist had done wonders and then ordered a glass of red wine. Like several years previously, the man threw the wine in the bartender's face. The bartender said, "I don't understand. You said the therapist did a great job!" The man said, "Yeah, now I know why I do it."

As an item of note on group process, this moment is a time to also open up and address issues of competition between group members. There may be some jockeying for position about which issues are more important to discuss. Is it ableism, sexual orientation, racism, sexism? At some point the group will also begin to unify and bond together against the group leader. This transition is both to be expected and healthy. In the CRAB groups, members asked questions like, "What's your job description again?" and "Do we need you?" As with all other group-dynamic issues, this one needs to be openly named and processed.

Putting the key points of resistance on the table for discussion does not automatically change people right away on all issues, or maybe even ever. It does, however, make us aware of our issues so that we can work with them to gain a better understanding of ourselves. Furthermore, our deepest friendships are with the people with whom we can get angry, get through the anger, and become closer as a result of sharing true feelings. This reality was true for the CRAB group members.

Point Six: Supporting the Development of New, Corrective, Bias-Free Behaviors

Even when individuals say, "I know I am behaving in hurtful ways," they often have no new behaviors to replace the old. Feelings of isolation, alienation, and frustration arise as a consequence of not knowing what to do or where to go for support. The fact that we *can* create environments for trying out new behaviors needs frequent emphasizing. There

is nothing worse than spending your life trying to do the right thing and then having somebody tell you that what you have been doing is wrong or hurtful. It makes it really difficult to go back into the classroom. We may wonder, "Should I go back to school and get another degree in another field?" or "Should I write to all the children I've ever had and tell them that I'm sorry?" That is not what this work is about. It is about saying to ourselves, "I am a good teacher. What I need to do is to begin to understand how to be a better teacher."

Once we understand the dynamics of how racism (and other forms of oppression) plays itself out in our interpersonal relationships, then we can start generalizing our experiences to other situations and thinking about different ways to respond. If we can identify, analyze, and change biased behaviors in the group, then we can begin to do the same in our classrooms, teacher trainings, community, and organizations.

The CRAB groups became laboratories for their members to develop and test new behaviors. Because the CRAB groups were small duplicates of the larger society, whatever occurred in the group was like a dress rehearsal. So, we tried to let it happen and encouraged people to put it on the table. Through this process we experienced and learned what a training participant, parent, co-worker, or child might never share with us—the way they really feel about similar issues.

Outcomes of the Six Point Cross-Cultural Group Development Process

Working through the many challenges at each point in the progression, and the returning/revisiting of each point in an ever-widening spiral supports both individual and group growth along several dimensions. These dimensions include

- personal growth that leads to greater self-awareness, healthy cultural identity, and more authentic, honest interpersonal relationships across cultures;
- the creation of group cohesion that reflects an interweaving of the different group members into a rich, synergetic whole, providing genuine support for its members; and

- professional skill development resulting in more effective, culturally sensitive teaching strategies with children and adults, as well as more effective advocacy and social change strategies.

The six stages of group development describe the process by which CRAB members made sense of their personal identities and collaborated with peers in the project to define and clarify their group membership. We acquired new skills for working with children and adults. Most important, we realized that there is a interaction between what we know and accept about ourselves and our ability to respectfully move others along toward a more just society. We learned how to live and work more congruently by closing the gap between what we preach and what we practice.

Finally, it is important to always keep in mind that as the CRAB group members engaged in their own growth through the dynamics of the group's developmental process, they also took what they were learning into their workplaces and began creating cross-cultural teams with other CRAB members to provide training for others. Then they brought back their work experiences to the group for feedback and reflection. Thus our approach involved a dynamic interaction between personal and professional growth. And the cycle was continuous. We met monthly to enhance our awareness, which led us to new behavior and new practices, which in turn led to new awareness. If we worked together in cross-cultural teams to provide training to others but didn't participate in our ongoing group process, it would have been difficult to get beyond superficial "tourist" teaching or interpersonal relationships with one another. If we participated in the group process but didn't engage in the training of others, we would have limited our learning opportunities for testing new perspectives, knowledge, and behaviors.

For early childhood educators who truly envision a society in which children have the right to a free, nonracist, nonsexist education that respects their traditions and cultures, a structure like that of the CRAB groups offers the environment in which the essential work of struggling through the four goals of culturally relevant anti-bias education can take place.

Resources
Pedersen, Paul. *A Handbook for Developing Multicultural Awareness.* Alexandria, VA: American Association for Counseling and Development, 1988.

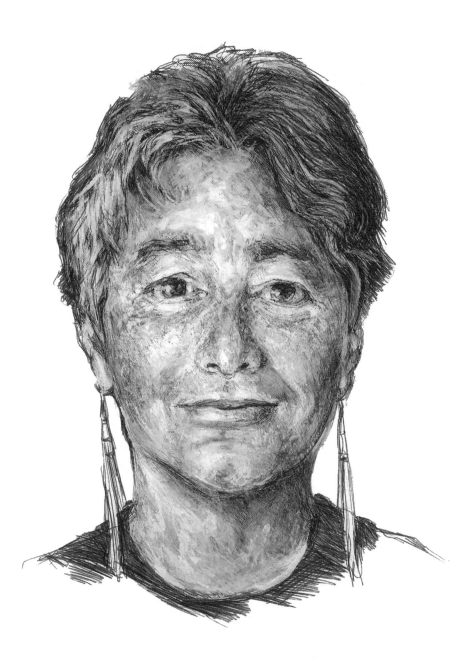

Louise Derman-Sparks

Chapter 6

Taking Action

*I had no idea when I refused to give up my seat on that
Montgomery bus that my small action would help put
an end to the segregation laws in the South. I only
knew that I was tired of being pushed around.*

—Rosa Parks, *My Story*

*A critical number of advocates of change can create a
preferential direction like the inner ordering of a
crystal or magnet that organizes the whole.*

—Ilya Prigogine, 1977 Nobel Peace Prize Winner

At its heart, culturally relevant anti-bias education is about creating a
more just, equitable, and caring society for all children. Thus, it is a part
of the broader movement for social justice in our society and in the
world. Educational and social change are a collaborative, community
processes requiring long-term action on many different levels. Each of
us brings a piece of the whole—and we need all the pieces not only to
see the full picture but also to see where our piece fits in. We also need
other people to sustain ourselves for doing the persistent, thoughtful
action that brings about change.

Kenneth Jones (see below) helped people in the CRAB groups get focused about their vision by posing the following scenario. Use it to clarify your vision.

Scenario:
So many years into the future, you have gotten all the things you have been struggling for. One morning, the families and children in your community invite you to walk around the community and early childhood programs to show you all that you have accomplished. What is there, what do you see, hear?

Here are some of our responses:

- "I see early childhood programs and communities that are beautiful and clean."
- "I hear many kinds of music and see many kinds of art."
- "I see communities that are free of poverty and have an abundance of resources."
- "I see people who live where they want. All cultural groups are seen everywhere. Multiple languages are spoken everywhere. And the retail stores reflect this diversity of cultures."
- "I see early childhood programs that extol all cultural groups, support all children's home languages, and teach children in culturally appropriate ways. The staff reflects the diversity of the children's communities."
- "I see peaceful people smiling, showing respect for one another, and cooperating rather than competing."

The courage to act for change springs from a clear vision of our destination. In a 1998 essay titled "The Importance of a Shared Vision," Kenneth Jones, an organizational consultant for community groups across the country, emphasizes the importance of having a clear vision by stating that "a vision is a positive and inspired picture of the future. It allows us to see what our community will look like after we achieve our goals. This tells us the direction and destination of our work. A clear shared vision helps us to reach out beyond today's struggles, issues, problems and stay focused on where we are going... [it] lets us know that what connects us is more important than what separates us."

It is a challenge to hold on to our visions when the work of getting there is so arduous and slow. Our children's needs are so great. We want to see results now, yet we have "inch by inch, row by row" outcomes. Taking action also depends on hope and faith in our capacity to work in community to build a more just world. As Dr. Martin Luther King Jr. so movingly made clear, "We've got some difficult days ahead. But it doesn't matter with me now. Because I've been to the mountain top . . . and I've seen the promised land. . . . I want you to know tonight, that we, as a people, will get to the promised land" (qtd. in Washington, 1986).

This chapter provides a framework for thinking about ways of working on culturally relevant anti–bias education in your early childhood programs and communities by examining the activities carried out by the members of the three pilot CRAB groups. This discussion is not intended as a recipe for replication but rather to provide examples of possibilities. Individuals came to our CRAB groups at different levels of experience and with varying confidence in their leadership skills. Some people were already out there doing community work or public policy activities. However, as Stacey York recalls, "I can remember many people saying that they weren't ready to go out. They didn't know enough. It was too scary. They were afraid of making a mistake. These fears stopped them from taking action at first. Eventually the attitude became 'Let's do it!' In fact, people became so active that we created a demand beyond our supply of time."

The Arenas of Action

Culturally relevant anti–bias education work, like all education and social change work, always takes place within specific community contexts. It is most successful when we do it within the various communities, small

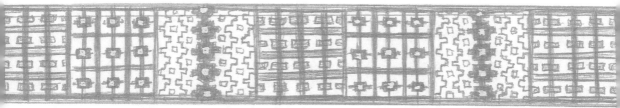

and large, in which we work and live. In these settings we have connections to people that enable us to assess what needs to be done, find others to work with us, devise culturally relevant strategies, and be accountable to the people with whom we work.

Each of us operates in many specific communities: families; neighborhoods; ethnic and cultural communities; faith-based institutions; our children's classrooms and schools; our workplaces; and local, state, and national levels of early childhood organizations and other advocacy groups. CRAB work is necessary in all of these arenas. The specific kind of work we choose to do at any given time reflects what is happening in the multiple communities to which we belong as well as our place within them. As one group member aptly commented, "My job and everything else I do provide numerous and daily opportunities to work on the issues. It is a way of life now, and very hard to separate individual events."

Working Within the Early Childhood System

Integrating culturally relevant anti-bias education into early childhood programs requires change in the many aspects of the early childhood *system* if it is to be sustained in any one area. This means we have to work collectively in the following areas: programs serving children and families, teacher training, resource and referral agencies, early childhood organizations, and all levels of government—city, state, and national. Changes in these multiple parts of the early childhood system also require changes in the attitudes, knowledge base, and behaviors of all players. Possible activities to create change span a wide spectrum, as illustrated in the following examples of CRAB group members' activities.

Work Directly with Children and Families

CRAB group members integrated culturally relevant and anti-bias approaches into practice with children in a variety of early childhood settings, including family day-care homes, Head Start programs, cooperative preschool and child care programs, YWCA child care centers, first grade classrooms, school-age child care programs, and parent-child classes.

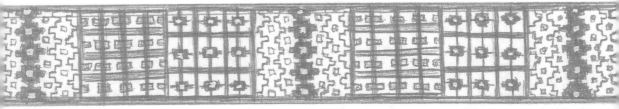

Individuals decided what to do in their own work settings, based on their own analysis of needs and possibilities, as well as the feedback from discussions with individual group members and the group as a whole. Activities with families included the following:

- Setting up a parent education/support class for Spanish speakers;
- Working with a support group for parents of Deaf children to add bilingual and bicultural criteria for Deaf children to the school district's individual evaluation profiles;
- Starting a support group for Native American parents; and
- Involving parents in writing "persona doll" stories for their children's preschool class.

Train and Raise Awareness among Practitioners Providing Direct Services to Children

One-time workshops that introduce people to culturally relevant anti-bias education concepts are usually the starting place for raising awareness and training practitioners. These steps take place in a variety of venues, such as in-services for staffs of early childhood programs or agencies, workshops at local and state conferences, and sessions at community colleges. Sometimes the workshop topic focuses on culturally relevant anti-bias issues, and sometimes these concepts are woven into workshops addressing other aspects of early childhood work (for example, classes on developmentally appropriate curriculum and conflict resolution for early childhood education public school teachers).

Requests for training workshops from early childhood programs and agencies were brought to the CRAB group as a whole. Decisions concerning who presented the workshops depended on individual interest, availability, and the group's sense of which group members were best suited for a particular audience. Each group also made choices about which local and state early childhood conferences it wanted to present workshops.

In a time span of two-and-a-half years, we estimated that CRAB members collectively disseminated the core ideas of culturally relevant anti-bias education to approximately 8,000 people through one-time

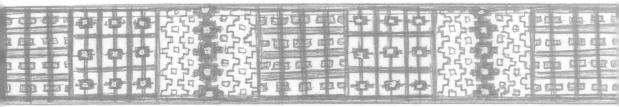

workshops. Practitioners working with children made up 40 percent of the workshop participants, directors and program coordinators accounted for 23 percent, assistant teachers and teacher aides made up 16 percent, parent educators and family advocates totaled 14 percent, and college instructors represented 7 percent.

However, one-time workshops are only the first step. They do not, for the most part, change practice. More long-term strategies that build ongoing relationships with practitioners are critical to producing real changes in programs and services for children. Some of the ways we were able to build ongoing relationships with practitioners included the following:

- setting up neighborhood and citywide early childhood teachers' support groups that met weekly or biweekly;
- integrating culturally relevant anti-bias education topics in weekly staff meetings and program trainings;
- setting up ethnic-specific teacher support groups to address issues pertinent to their children and families; and
- initiating courses at community colleges.

Work with Trainers and College Educators

This work also requires a variety of long-term activities. Some of those used by members of the CRAB groups included the following:

- helping to set up and participate on a committee to rewrite the early childhood education curriculum at a community college to be inclusive, relevant, and committed to anti-bias principles;
- revising policies at a community college to require that all students take a diversity-awareness course;
- forming a diversity committee at a community college to improve the curriculum by integrating anti-bias principles into staff recruitment, hiring, and support policies;
- working with a statewide project to ensure that culturally relevant anti-bias practices are fully integrated into in-service training curriculum for child care and preschool teachers;

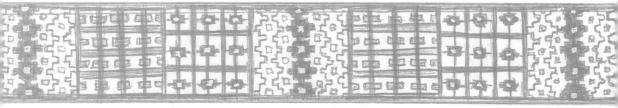

- helping to set up a task force to work on long-term diversity and equity issues and training across the state; and
- providing training for 2,000 staff of the statewide Early Childhood and Family Education and Learning Readiness programs.

Influence Policy Decisions by Early Childhood and Governmental Agencies

This work sets the stage for giving legitimacy to training practitioners on culturally relevant anti-bias issues and for making changes within community colleges and other organizations that provide training. Again there are several ways that CRAB members influenced policy decisions:

- working with the Seattle Department of Family and Youth Services to develop new licensing policies requiring diversity training for providers, culturally relevant curriculum with children, and a new tool to assess centers' use of culturally relevant anti-bias principles;
- co-chairing a statewide committee to develop an early childhood education career development system, making sure that provisions for career development of people of color and general anti-bias practices were incorporated into the initial plan;
- facilitating the textbook selection committee for the New Orleans Public Schools, which reviews criteria for addressing multicultural and anti-bias issues in reading; and
- meeting with the cultural diversity committee of the Minneapolis Day Care Association to discuss coordinating Latino and Southeast Asian outreach efforts between MCDA and Child Care Resources.

Working within our Family and Cultural Communities

The original goals of the CRAB project focused more on creating change within the early childhood system and less on other parts of our communities that care for and educate children. However, we came to realize that individuals' families and cultural communities are also essential arenas of culturally relevant anti-bias education work.

Family

The family is often the first context in which we begin trying out new perspectives and ideas. Indeed, our work has a great impact on the members of our families, both directly and indirectly. The following examples illustrate some of the many possibilities.

> Empowering our own children:
> "I've been talking with my son, who has a physical disability, about what I am learning in the CRAB group and doing at work. Recently he told me, 'I am so glad you are in this group, because it makes me feel stronger standing up for myself when kids tease me.'"

> Influencing our children's school experiences:
> "I'm serving as parent advisor to the Students and Teachers Against Racism club at my daughter's middle school. At first I was concerned that she might not want me to do this, but she is actually proud that I am."

> "I'm working with my child's kindergarten teacher to create a good collection of books showing family diversity. The teacher is open to the idea, but she would not have done it on her own."

> Influencing family members:
> "At first my husband wasn't so sure about what I was doing with this group. Recently at a picnic a colleague made a racist kind of remark. My husband responded, "You better go talk to my wife about that."

While some people viewed such conversations with family members as an informal part of their work, others considered these interactions an important part of their efforts. People in the latter category felt that we should more purposefully include discussions about our families in the CRAB meetings.

Cultural Communities

The cultural communities to which we belong are another critical context for our work. Children and families are served by many community

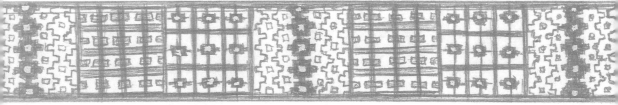

institutions in addition to early childhood programs. These services may either support or hinder culturally relevant and anti-bias approaches. Moreover, changing early childhood education cannot occur in a vacuum. It requires the support of the wider communities in which the families we serve live. Young children need continued opportunities to develop strong identities, appreciate and value differences, pracitce critical thinking, and take responsibility for standing up for justice.

The following statements by CRAB group members illustrate the ways in which members worked in their various cultural community contexts beyond the early childhood system:

> "Having been active in the Girl Scouts for several years, I decided to set up a Girl Scouts Leadership Team for Diversity in my suburban town and to do anti-bias training for leaders and staff of the Girl Scout summer camp."

> "The Latina CRAB members joined with other Latino community leaders to create a Children and Family Latino Advocacy Task Force. The goals are to develop an action agenda to address all of the various neglected needs of Latina/Latino children and families."

> "A few of us in the Seattle CRAB group learned about an anti-racist group called People of Europe American Dissent from European American members in the New Orleans CRAB group and started a similar group in our city."

> "I'm working with the American Friends Service Committee Gay/Lesbian Youth Task Force to educate and provide counseling and support to high school students and do teacher education."

> "I joined the Minnesota Council of Churches anti-racism project as a representative from my church."

> "Several people of color in the Minneapolis/St. Paul CRAB group designed a proposal and received a grant from the Minnesota Department of Early Childhood Education to build a state network of early childhood educators who are people of color."

Working in Local, State, Regional, and National Early Childhood Organizations

Ultimately change in early childhood programs only happens if the people providing direct services to children and families believe in and make the changes in their daily practice. However, work for culturally relevant anti-bias ideals and approaches must also take place in the various professional organizations that support early childhood practitioners. Examples of such professional organizations include the National Association for the Education of Young Children (NAEYC) and its affiliates, the National Family Day Care Association (NFDCA), and the National Association of Child Care Resource and Referral Agencies (NACCRRA). These organizations determine and promote the criteria for quality care and educational practice, recruit new practitioners and build leadership within the field, disseminate new theoretical and practical knowledge, and influence public policy. By virtue of these roles these organizations can create possibilities for and have the resources to support culturally relevant anti-bias work. Therefore they are also essential arenas for work at the local, state, regional, and national levels.

State AEYC affiliates were a major focus of attention for all three CRAB groups. The Seattle group's efforts were particularly effective because members developed the most extensive long-term plan. They made working within the Washington AEYC a priority and focused on electing people of color to the state board, which was traditionally white. CRAB members of color volunteered to run for the various offices on the board and were elected. From those elected positions, they developed a new mission statement that articulated a stronger commitment to diversity and equity and called on local chapters to develop plans for creating a more diverse membership and leadership congruent with the revised mission. As members and chair of the Washington AEYC conference committees, CRAB members established a culturally relevant anti-bias education track as a regular part of the state conference, for which participants are now able to receive college credit. They also developed a proposal for and received a grant from the NAEYC to organize training and support for implementing the new NAEYC position paper on "Cultural and Linguistic Diversity."

Members of all the CRAB groups also worked within several other early childhood organizations. In addition to working with the State Director's Associations and the National Black Child Development Institute, CRAB members persuaded the NACCRRA to participate in a weekend of anti-racism training. The Ecumenical Child Care Network national steering committee strengthened its anti-bias guidelines in its self-study guide due to the work of CRAB members. And CRAB members successfully joined with others to move the national conference of the National Association for Family Day Care out of Colorado to protest the state's new anti-gay legislation.

Making Choices

The need and possibilities for doing culturally relevant anti-bias education are greater than even a group of committed individuals can take on at any point in time. Making decisions about what to do in a given period of time as an individual, and in collaboration with others, is an ongoing challenge. One advantage of being part of a group is not having to do everything. As one CRAB member aptly explained, "There are some issues for which I don't want to get on the bandwagon, but I see the other members feeling strongly about them and I can support that. If everybody can feel a level of comfort in knowing their roles in any type of movement, then anything can work."

A group provides the place for brainstorming and examining possibilities for taking action as an individual, with group members, and with others in our various communities. To do this effectively requires analysis of the needs and the social, political, and economic dynamics of the institutions and communities in which we work. Choices about what to do and where to do it are greatly enriched by group members' bringing information and perspectives from various sectors of early childhood work and from various cultural communities. Networking among the group members opens up strategic possibilities and resources beyond what any one person might have at her disposal. Hearing about one

> "Moving ahead on one specific choice of action sometimes has a snowballing effect that opens up new possibilities that weren't envisioned beforehand. The different areas where we are taking action all overlap. A group member has lunch with someone and a training request results. Or we are asked to consult about organizational change and now we have several new activities to carry out. Or from our group discussions we decide to work to create a law that requires training in cultural dynamics. When the law is passed we've got this need for trainers and training on a whole new scale. The moral is you make a change in one place and that results in creating new needs in other places."
>
> —Stacey York,
> Minneapolis/St. Paul
> Co-coordinator

another's experiences leads to new ideas for individual and team activities.

To make effective choices about where and how to work, the group must take into account the group's resources for any specific activity: the knowledge, skills, connections, comfort levels, availability, and time constraints of group members. Furthermore, the group also must consider where members will be most effective, given their particular backgrounds, experience, and strengths. We found it helpful to think about the following questions:

1. With what communities and issues am I most interested in working?
2. In what community or communities am I best suited to work? How will being who I am (my ethnicity, culture, and my early childhood role) be perceived by a specific population? Where am I most likely to connect?
3. On what issues do I have knowledge and skills, and with whom might I work to best serve a particular population?

With what communities and issues am I most interested in working?

Figuring out your responses to this question means taking into account your preferred areas of work, the kind of work you like to do (for example, informal discussions, workshops, consulting, organizational and policy change, and so on), and the diversity and equity issues to which you are most drawn. To some extent choices about where to focus your energy depend on the dynamics of the larger community in which you live and work. However, individual preferences are also a fac-

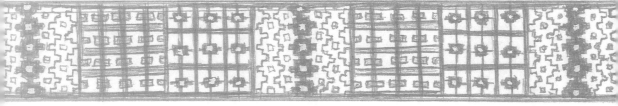

tor. We generally work most effectively in places where we feel the most passion about creating change.

In what community or communities am I best suited to work? How will being who I am (my ethnicity, culture, and my early childhood role) be perceived by a specific population? Where am I most likely to connect?

In general, it is most effective to work in the communities to which one has ties and to think carefully ahead of time about how one is likely to be received in that community. For example, one Minneapolis/St. Paul CRAB group member explained that "in rural areas where change is viewed with wariness and white people's experience with diverse populations is often more limited or restricted than in urban areas, a diversity trainer is viewed with a large dose of suspicion right off the bat. What I do to build a rapport with participants is to share my own background as a farm kid and a Christian, allowing them to see me as someone like them who has some information and resources they can use."

In a another situation, a team of two CRAB members—one European American and one Native American—agreed to do a workshop for a group of child care and Head Start workers that was approximately 70 percent European American and 30 percent Native American. The Native American trainer from the CRAB group was reluctant to work with a mixed audience such as this one, preferring to focus within her own cultural community. During the workshop, she stated her belief that it wasn't okay for children who aren't Native American to learn most Native American dances because it does not show respect and isn't authentic. Some of the Native American individuals in the audience disagreed with her—stating that at least it was a sign of interest in Native American culture—and then supported a European American workshop participant American who spoke to her with hostility. This really upset her, but she didn't want to start an argument with other Native Americans in that setting. She thought that the Native Americans needed to have this kind of discussion with one another first. It was very painful for her to be out there by herself without support from others in her cultural community.

On what issues do I have knowledge and skills, and with whom might I work to best serve a particular population?

Working in teams is often essential and always desirable. Teams can reflect a variety of types of diversity. Cross-ethnic teams are usually what first comes to mind, and when a community is culturally diverse, it is the preferred way of working. Cross-cultural teams model new ways of interacting and are better suited to interpret needs and dynamics when working with culturally mixed communities. When working with culturally homogeneous groups, another kind of diversity on the team may be more effective, especially if the objective of the training or consultation is cultural empowerment. In such cases, it may be more effective to have teams that differ in age, gender, class, physical ability, or sexual orientation.

Taking Stock

Good planning requires regular reflection on what has been accomplished in order to plan what needs to come next. Unfortunately it is much easier to know this in our heads than to actually practice it. As Sharon Henry (the co-coordinator of the Minneapolis/St. Paul CRAB group) puts it, "Evaluation has gotten such a bad name because it's been used as a tool by people in power to hold back resources. But *we* must use it as a tool to continually improve our own work. What we do is too critical for it to be an afterthought or to happen by accident."

Regular evaluation of both our outreach work and the group's internal dynamics enables us to uncover and pay attention to any problems that have developed. It also helps us realistically see what we have accomplished toward short- and long-term objectives, and where we have made "small changes." (Having evaluation procedures and documented data is also useful for writing funding proposals!) Periodically evaluating our work involves documenting our activities to get the full picture of what is happening and identifying what activities have been successful in relation to the goals of the group. It involves determining what is lacking and where new directions, strategies, and activities are needed. And, of course, it involves modifying current activities and plan-

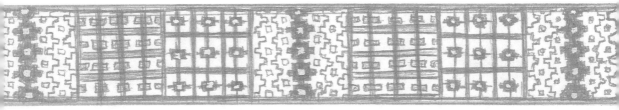

ning further actions based on the results of this evaluation. There are many ways to document what group members are doing. The CRAB groups created methods of documenting activities that worked for them, which included keeping track of activities in early childhood programs and community groups, keeping track of the internal group dynamics, and assessing the impact of training workshops and other activities.

Keeping Track of Activities in Early Childhood Programs and Community Groups

- One group performed interviews in dyads at the beginning of each monthly meeting and wrote down one another's responses. These notes were kept in a folder.
- Two groups used individual activity logs. Each person filled out a new sheet during the monthly meeting. This record was available at each meeting.
- In addition, all three groups used the technique of making a web diagram of the group's activities every six months.

Keeping Track of the Internal Group Dynamics

- One group used group journals. Each week a few people took the journal home to record their experiences and thoughts.
- Another group took individual turns being a process observer of the group's dynamics at the monthly meetings.
- The third group periodically interviewed one another about what was working and not working and what each person wanted from the rest of the group to keep growing.

Assessing the Impact of Training Workshops and other Activities

- All of the groups developed and used evaluation forms for participants in their workshops.
- Each group developed and used a self-evaluation form for group members to fill out after workshops.

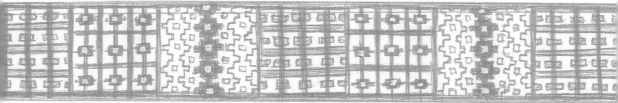

◆ Each group developed an oral or written questionnaire to get feedback from the early childhood community and various cultural communities who were aware of the CRAB group's work.

Documenting and collecting data is only the first step. What we do with this information is critical. The next steps involve reflecting on the data in relation to the group's mission, goals, and objectives, as well as planning further action based on those reflections. It is essential that the evaluation cycle be completed by bringing the conclusions back into the group's discussion. This may result in modifying aspects of what you are currently doing as well as developing new strategies and activities. For example, toward the end of the second year, several people of color in two of the CRAB groups expressed concerns that they were not doing enough within communities of color. With this in mind, the groups reexamined where they had been doing outreach work, and it became clear that the majority of training requests had come from programs primarily serving either European American children or ethnically mixed groups. It also became clear that the focus on work within early childhood organizations also meant working within the mainstream culture. While everyone agreed that this work was essential, people felt that the balance had become too skewed. To begin to fix this imbalance, two new projects were initiated.

The Minneapolis CRAB group first set up an all-day workshop for early childhood people of color, titled "A Time for Ourselves," which was held the day before that year's MNAEYC conference. Next, a group consisting of people of color, white people, and several members of the CRAB group wrote a grant proposal to the Minnesota Department of Human Services to create a group called Early Childhood Professionals of Color (ECPC). Its purpose was to provide an environment for people of color to build a network of support, address issues of racism and self-determination, and develop leadership opportunities. While several CRAB members served on its steering committee and became part of the network, ECPC was set up as a separate group.

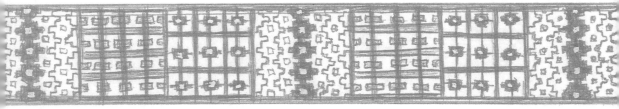

In Seattle the CRAB group came up with another strategy for increasing work within communities of color. The group organized neighborhood classes in child development and child care, focusing on neighborhoods with a high concentration of Latina/Latinos and African Americans. These classes were the result of a collaboration among a number of organizations, including the city of Seattle Comprehensive Child Development programs, the Seattle Central Community College, the School's Out Consortium, the Seattle–King County Department of Public Health, the African America Child Care Task Force, and the Latino Child Care Task. CRAB members participated as staff or members in all but one of these organizations and were instrumental in bringing them together to sponsor this project. Students in the classes also have the chance to continue their education at the community college. These classes are significantly increasing the number of child care practitioners of color getting needed training and access to further education.

Taking stock of a group's activities also includes taking the pulse of individual members. Working on culturally relevant anti-bias education is demanding in itself. In addition, most of the CRAB group members were also doing "overtime" beyond their actual job hours. As CRAB related work increased, people began to experience fatigue and frustration with the slow pace of change. At first, members experienced these feelings as theirs alone. However, during a retreat of the women of color in the Minnesota group, the issue finally emerged as a group concern. People recognized that they were so busy taking care of others they were not taking time to rejuvenate themselves. Their discussion raised our awareness. We all realized that we couldn't be effective if we were too emotionally drained or physically exhausted. It is important to build in some fun as part of the group's time together, especially during retreats, and to help each other find ways to get personal rest and recreation.

A Personal Note
I have been an activist for social change for a good part of my fifty-eight years, and I expect to continue for the rest of my life. I see my work as something like the marriage vow—to persist in for better or worse. What

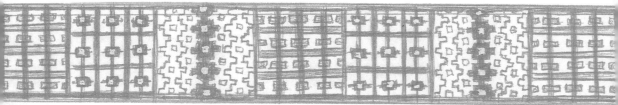

keeps me hanging in? What helps me accept the great amounts of time and energy that go into seemingly small results? Of most help is knowing that I do not do this work alone. As Sharon Cronin reminds us in chapter 2, each of us builds on the work done by people who came before us and will be continued by others after us. When I get frustrated with changes being small, I hum a line from "Garden Song" by Dave Mallet: "Inch by inch, row by row, gonna make my garden grow." This is the nature of working on culturally relevant anti-bias education. Each small act and change contributes to the garden growing a little more each day.

When I get tangled up in fears that I don't know the right solutions to the challenges I face, I recall the following passage from one of Rainer Maria Rilke's *Letters to a Young Poet:*

> Live the questions now. Perhaps you will gradually, without noticing it, live along some distant day into the answer.

Ultimately I return to my vision of what all children deserve to have. Then I feel reenergized and ready to go again.

Resources

Jones, Kenneth. "The Importance of a Shared Vision." In *The Web: Newsletter of the Culturally Relevant Anti-Bias Education Leadership Network*. April 1998.

Washington, James, ed. *The Testament of Hope: The Essential Writing and Speeches of Martin Luther King, Jr.* San Francisco: Harper, 1986.

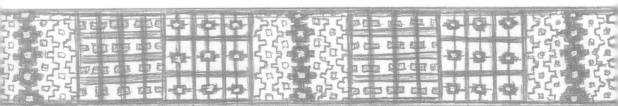

Sharon Cronin, Sharon Henry, Cirecie Olatunji

Chapter 7

Moving the Center: Reflections of the Coordinators of Color

Early on in discussions about writing this book, the three of us came to realize that we shared an uneasiness about proceeding. Something was missing. We decided that we needed do an additional critical analysis of the lessons of the CRAB project from our perspective as people of color. The three of us held a reflective summit as the coordinators of color involved in the CRAB project and the authors of color writing this book. The thinking and discussion that took part during that weekend influenced our writing throughout the book. This chapter focuses specifically on the insights from that weekend and our conclusions about the lessons of the CRAB project as people of color.

Even before we began writing, the three of us had become concerned that some of the people of color in our CRAB groups were having less dialogue and doing less developmental work within their own cultural communities than they were doing within primarily European American settings. We felt disjointed in our thinking and discussions with one another and with other CRAB participants about doing culturally relevant anti-bias work with children of color, their families, and their communities. The work we were doing through the CRAB groups and the dialogues in which we participated were often not consistent with our cultural frameworks and worldviews. The CRAB groups' meeting agenda and training plans didn't always fit the reality we were observing and living. We took some specific steps within the CRAB groups to address these concerns. However, we realized, as we looked back over our work in the process of writing this book, that the groups had operated throughout much of the CRAB project in ways preventing the culturally relevant aspect of our work for people of color from moving forward as we needed it to. Therefore, while all the CRAB participants got better at identifying European American racism and finding specific tools to help European Americans work at undoing racism, we did not have a parallel toolbox for supporting people of color in undoing the effects of racism in their own lives and communities.

Eurocentric Discourse as Default Mode

The three of us came up with a name for the dynamic we were analyzing and critiquing. We called it "default mode," borrowing from computer language where the term signifies standard formatting instructions. Because European American culture is the dominant culture in our society (the one with the institutionalized power to assert itself as the standard for discourse and behavior), default mode in our context meant that CRAB meetings were more closely aligned with the needs, interests, preferences and comfort of European American participants than they were with those of the participants of color. This reality affected the style of communication, language used, structure, and pacing of meetings, assigning of importance to agenda items, and even the meeting locations. We came to realize that unless we took active steps to change the focus, priorities, content, and mode of discourse in the CRAB groups, it automatically operated in the Eurocentric default mode. This was true even with very aware and well-meaning group members, whether European American or people of color. And maintaining a shifted center (avoiding the default mode) required constant attention. It could be established for a particular meeting, but unless the same efforts were applied to the next event, we would again find ourselves using the default mode. As people of color participating in collaborative progressive work such as our CRAB groups, we shared responsibility for allowing the "default mode" of communication to operate for as long as it did. It wasn't until we finally identified and named it that we could seriously address our concerns.

By reflecting critically on the work the groups were doing in each project city, we were able to identify ways that the "default mode" was also operating in relation to whom the CRAB project was primarily serving. For example, the primary way groups were providing training tended to serve European Americans better. A majority of training requests to the CRAB groups tended to come from early childhood programs primarily serving European American children. That is also where most resources for training existed. Often communities of color are not in charge of the training resources in the area, and many programs serving primarily communities of color did not have training budgets at all. Moreover, the style of providing training on issues of culturally relevant anti-bias approaches to education that requires going to a resource center to get training isn't necessarily appropriate for recruiting participants and educating professionals and parents within communities of color. Not all cultural communities approach family and community development from an isolated time period or stage in development. People may not organize for change or for development around "early childhood" as a separate, unique period in a family's life. The approach in some of our communities is much more holistic and intergenerational. In most cases, learning how to be a competent parent (even a culturally relevant anti-bias parent) within communities of color didn't happen in the come-to-a-parent-education-class model. We also discussed the trust issues and hesitancy many parents of color have with outside interference in their family matters—particularly from agencies or institutions associated primarily with the dominant European American culture.

The effectiveness of our training for people and communities of color was thus affected by the CRAB groups' Eurocentric default mode of functioning.

Moving the Center

Getting clearer about our "default mode" of operating in the CRAB groups and work was the first step in our critical analysis. Then we

Recently I was conducting training with faculty at a prestigious undergraduate institution. My role was to help participants become more sensitive to graduate students of color in their program. During the workshop, the most vehement resistance to my perspective came from the person of color who had asked me to do the training in the first place. I realized that if she were a white person, I would have been prepared with a whole bag of ways to work with the situation. But I was stymied about how to deal with a person of color in this situation. I knew there were different dynamics, issues, and politics to address, and it was clear to me what not to do in that broader context. I was aware that many things could have been going through this woman's mind. Perhaps I was bringing up issues that she did not want addressed in this mixed group. Maybe she had felt threatened, or possibly the training opened up something very painful within her ethnic identity development. I briefly flashed on some potential strategies and ways to respond. But it was clear to me then that I did not have the benefit of collective dialogue and reflection on specific strategies for people of color. I did not have a selection of training techniques to draw upon in that moment. I realized at that moment that we had made a crucial error in overfocusing on European American dynamics and not paying attention to the issue of working with internalized oppression and other dynamics related to people of color.

—Cirecie Olatunji, New Orleans Coordinator

moved on to the work of figuring out how to translate new thinking into actual behavior. We called this step "moving the center." This meant opening up our group meetings to all of the voices present to allow group members to "stay in their right minds" (a sense of being deeply connected to one's cultural identity and being able to resist racism from that position of strength). We found that we did not have to do meetings the same old way, and that we needed to break loose from "default mode" by posing and solving questions such as the following, which are particularly important to participants of color:

- What would meetings look like if they were consistent with cultural styles you are familiar with?
- How are important meetings conducted in your cultural community?
- What would you like to add to our meetings?
- What languages should be used?
- What cultural arts and aesthetic qualities would you like present? How do you open a meeting in your community? How do you bring closure?
- How will you allow for the cultural styles and languages of other cultural groups?

As people of color working in European American and multiracial groups, we found it essential to learn skills and strategies for "moving the center." Shifting who was in charge of setting up the meeting—who organized the time, space, and content—was key to moving the center. So, too, was paying attention to the first languages of group members. The chosen style of communication influences the sociocultural center of a gathering or a group. Even if participants are fully bilingual, they tire of communicating exclusively in Standard English. Sometimes a person just wants to express a thought in her own language or communication style. It has been said that a translation is like the backside of a tapestry—it is just not the same as the original communication, and it does not have the same eloquence or aesthetics. In addition, another language may not contain words for a particular concept that a meeting participant wants to express. When English is used exclusively to conduct meetings, the burden of coping with these difficul-

"Communication between human beings is also the basis and process of evolving culture . . . culture embodies those moral, ethical, and aesthetic values, the set of spiritual eyeglasses, through which they come to view themselves and their place in the universe. Values are the basis of a people's identity, their sense of particularity as members of the human race. All this is carried by language. Language as culture is the collective memory bank of a people's experience in history."

—Ngogi wa Thiong'o

ties falls entirely on the people for whom English is not a first or preferred language.

Some of our CRAB participants from Head Start and early childhood education programs became very skilled at holding meetings and training sessions using translation equipment. In one case, the presenter spoke in Spanish for part of the session and English for another part of the session. A translator used a microphone and radio transmitter to send the translated message to participants wearing headphones. Both English- and Spanish-speaking participants had headphones that they used when the presenter was speaking in the language they didn't speak. This allowed the meeting to proceed more quickly and smoothly than if the presenter had to stop and wait for the translation after everything she said. Since everyone had headphones, it balanced the power dynamic and value of the languages. And Spanish speakers felt just as comfortable asking questions since the question was automatically translated for the English speakers regardless of the language the presenter used.

We found that it was necessary to take steps to ensure that we kept cultural relevancy in the center of our internal group dynamics as well as in our outreach work. That meant always monitoring the process and ourselves, including asking ourselves what was getting in the way of our doing this. We needed to continue asking ourselves, "What are the processes for facilitating political, social, and cultural change in early childhood communities of color?" We had to address the issues for people of color within our groups as well as those between our groups and the broader communities of color as we carried out the tasks of creating culturally relevant anti-bias environments for young children. This problem was only broached in the CRAB groups. For example, creating training modules on how to work with early childhood communities of color must be a primary area of ongoing CRAB work.

Another critical question for ongoing culturally relevant anti-bias work is how to get more buy-in to the CRAB approach from communities of color. We still need to understand better what factors prevented the CRAB groups from doing more in an area in which we desperately need to conduct work. For example, there are many people who are imple-

menting Afrocentric or other culturally specific programs who do not have a significant background in curriculum development. Many individuals also do not accept the need of addressing any other anti-bias issues or introducing learning about diversity other than their own. On the other hand, we have lots of people who are seasoned educators who don't want to hear anything about culture, or who accept the need for an anti-bias approach but not a culturally relevant one. To do the vital work of bringing anti-bias and culturally relevant thinking together, we must find our voices as people of color.

Learning to Stay in Our "Right Minds"

The struggles of the men and women in the Culturally Relevant Anti-Bias Leadership Project taught us lessons useful for white people as well as people of color. In order to do culturally relevant work, educators need to begin the process of deconstructing an identity shaped within a racist society. For people of color, this means minimizing the tendency to internalize the oppression and conduct pro-racist acts. So often people of color consciously or subconsciously act in the interests of the dominant group. For white people this means reducing the tendency to drown out or dismiss the voices of others who are different from the mainstream—for example, people who are insisting there really are other models of child development and styles of learning related to a child's culture.

We each have our own personal life-time work to do around the issues of oppressions in our society. Because culture is socially constructed, it is important to reflect with others who are both similar and dissimilar from ourselves to understand more clearly the role of oppressions in our individual lives and in our society at large. The CRAB groups became living laboratories, safe havens to explore one's own identity without doing it at the expense of others, to become challenged and supported as an educator and as a person. In doing this work, we created a learning community that modeled an approach to humanizing ourselves and engaged in ongoing corrective human development.

Remaining rooted in and working from within our cultural communities was also crucial to "staying in our right minds" and to working with others without losing our center and our acceptability to our communities. We had to ask ourselves, "Who am I? What is my role in all of this work?" "Which aspects do I especially want to promote?" "Am I a 'bridge builder'?" "Am I a leader, or am I a worker?" "Is the focus of my work to be an outstanding teacher in the classroom, out in my community, or in the larger early childhood community? Or, do I want to do some combination of all three?" As teachers or trainers, we are always influencing and advocating for our communities. The CRAB groups became a vehicle in which we could develop the skills needed to rebuild communities, regardless of the community in which we served.

Undoing Oppression in Culturally Relevant Ways

When Sharon Cronin agreed to be a part of this project, she asked that "Culturally Relevant" be added to the name since her experience of "undoing" oppression within early childhood education centered around the bilingual multicultural child development movement. At first, these two notions—creating culturally relevant programs for children of color and anti-bias education to help children recognize, think critically about, and act against bias—were thought of as two different approaches or separate concepts. Once we moved the center of our discourse to focus on the needs of communities of color, we worked through our understanding of how these two parts of our project title come together. They are not separate terms for us now. As we revisited the work of the CRAB groups, underlining the importance of culture in working on anti-bias issues, looking again at "culturally specific" in light of the CRAB work, and reaffirming the historic legacy of resistance of people of color and white people in North America, we turned more comfortably to figuring out how to appropriately incorporate the valuable techniques and strategies contained in *Anti-Bias Curriculum: Tools for Empowering Young Children* into our thinking about the needs of children and communities of color.

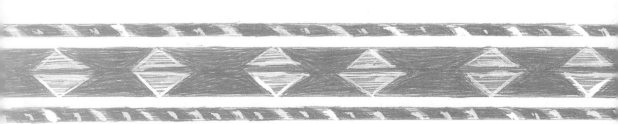

Another key shift in our thinking was to place anti-bias education in the historical context of resistance by people of color to racism in the Americas. We realized we must begin with the first people in the Americas who resisted the imposition of racism on them, including the racist ideology that constructed the idea of racial categories using skin color, hair texture, facial features, and body size as group markers and then held one category superior and all others inferior. We must honor the Native American and African ancestors who escaped the institution of slavery and formed independent communities. We must recognize people of European background who opposed the institution of slavery and racial oppression. We must all know many examples of resistance in the Americas over the past 500 years.

We also focused more on the meaning of the proverb "It takes a village to raise a child." While this wonderful yet misused West African proverb has been overused to the point of becoming a cliché, empty of meaning, the concept behind it is critical to the development of children of color and European American children. We must recognize that part of the problem we face is that many of our children are not being raised within a supporting village. Too many families—especially single-parent families and young families—find themselves isolated and without support. Many of them do not have access to the legacy of parenting strategies for raising children in their cultural group.

At the core of a village approach to raising children is the acknowledgment that children need the ongoing attention, love, guidance, and vigilance parents and other significant adults have to offer. Moreover, those needs are best met in an intergenerational context. The following quote, taken from an "Akwesasne Notes" poster of a grandmother and little toddler walking down a road, best characterizes the idea: "The life cycle of creation is endless. We watch the seasons come and go, life into life forever. The child becomes parent, who then becomes our respected elder. Life is so sacred—it is good to be a part of all this." This returns to an idea raised previously regarding the way focusing only on early childhood may be a backward approach to parent education, family development, and culturally relevant anti-bias work. Although we have decided to focus our work on the development and education of young children, we are very aware that they are a part of families, neighborhoods, and communities. CRAB work is strengthened when it includes the extended family. It flows better. It feels more whole.

We see great value in Asian Americans and Pacific Islanders, African Americans, Latinos, and Native Americans talking about their traditional child rearing practices and value structures as a part of reflecting on viable ways of caring for children (if parents need child care services) and supporting the collective development of their children. They are in the best position to reflect on how to support the construction of a healthy identity for their children. They can identify what challenges, dangers, and risks they feel their children will encounter. These parents can share strategies and ideas from past experiences.

For example, in the Seattle area a needs assessment was conducted based on community participation. Responsible for organizing this assessment was the African American Child Care Task Force (AAC-CTF), a few of whose members were also part of the Seattle CRAB group, working with support from the National Black Child Development Institute. The group observed early childhood programs and interviewed child care providers serving large numbers of African American children to determine what needs existed for quality care and what the barriers were to obtaining it. The information was shared in a community summit attended by teachers, community leaders, providers, and parents who had created an action agenda to address the needs identified. The AACCTF were very strategic in bringing attention to the document. Nobody got a copy before the release party and press conference! Because the group was so unified and focused, its efforts were very effective and many of the recommendations of the action agenda were implemented by the city child care subsidy programs, the licensing agencies, and the local community colleges. Later, again with a few members from the Seattle CRAB group participating, a newly formed Latino Child Care Task Force followed this example and conducted peer interviews of Latino parents and child care and education programs. The AACCTF supported the development and success of the next group, who in turn supported the beginning of the Asian and Pacific Island Child Care Task Force. The ethnic-specific task force proved to be an effective model for "moving the center" and for allowing the voices of people of color to come forward and find a path for addressing culturally relevant child care issues. Perhaps even more important was the incredible collaborative leadership that emerged.

These task forces showed us that it is so important to use the knowledge gained from the parents, grandparents, and other caregivers in our communities to challenge the norms of early childhood education. These norms were generally created by middle-class European American women and men, based on the experiences and wisdom of *their* communities. Many of these developmental norms, and the recommended practices based on them, don't fit for all cultural groups. When they are used as teaching guidelines or evaluating measures of children, families, or programs in communities of color, they interfere with the healthy development of children and families.

Another example of exploring ways to undo oppression in culturally relevant ways comes from an action research project conducted by a team of African American, Latino, and European American students studying at Pacific Oaks College Northwest under the guidance of Sharon Cronin. From the data collected by interviewing parents and teachers, the team conceptualized ten principles of early childhood education that reflected the integral joining of culturally relevant and anti-bias perspectives. It began with a question that surfaced in class. The students knew that culturally relevant educational strategies are generally effective with students of color. The question was whether they could have an educational program that was culturally relevant for two cultural groups. The students decided to focus their efforts on African American and Latino children. Following are the ten ideas they developed as a result of the study. Although the suggestions are specific to four- to seven-year-old African American and Latino children, the concepts can be applied to other situations.

1. The ideal educational environment for four- to seven-year-old African American and Latino children reflects positive cultural images, is culturally relevant, and has an "everyday" natural cultural continuity.

2. Racial discrimination can be addressed and its potential scars prevented by caring adults who provide African American and Latino children with the opportunity and guidance to develop skills or strategies for survival, and who resist efforts to separate the children from their cultural, linguistic, and familial backgrounds.

3. Young African American and Latino children benefit from validation of the home language and daily contact with caring adults who model the use of their home language in social interaction and in the school setting.

4. Involving and creating partnerships with parents and community is central to developing culturally relevant teaching strategies.

5. Establishing a "critical mass" of children in a language or cultural group is a key dimension of culturally specific approaches to teaching; simultaneous culturally specific approaches consider critical mass as well as within-group linguistic and cultural variance. Critical mass means having enough of the same language speakers to create a language community within the classroom and providing enough anti-bias guidance and intervention on the part of the teacher to address discrimination based on culture or language.

6. Culturally relevant teaching has an "everydayness" inclusion of culture, provides avenues for the transmission of cultural knowledge and traditional literacy, supports the dynamic negotiation of present culture, and involves highly skilled adults from the cultural and linguistic backgrounds of the children and families.

7. Adults working with young children may have to process issues regarding their own internalized oppression, feelings of being unqualified, and lack of awareness of the most appropriate educational context for children of color. These issues require critical analysis and self-reflection, guidance and modeling, and theoretical and professional development.

8. Primary barriers to providing quality culturally relevant educational environments to African American and Latino

children include lack of resources, materials, and teachers; an unwillingness on the part of teachers and administrators to address the issues; and other forms of systemic cultural oppression and racism.

9. Once children of color are established in their own language and cultural systems, as well as their own communities, developing cross-literacy is valuable, appropriate, and necessary.

10. Simultaneous culturally specific approaches to teaching young African American and Latino children help children develop skills for functioning in many cultures—their own, one another's, and mainstream U.S. culture.

Taking Care of Ourselves: Balance, Sustainability, and Accountability

We learned that we needed to take care of ourselves and use our collective talents and energy more strategically. Here Cirecie describes a retreat she conducted with the people of color in one CRAB group that illustrates this lesson:

I saw a room full of warriors—warriors who were so busy doing for others that they left no room for themselves or for working with one another. They had slotted me in between 11:30 and 12:30 and it's like they were saying to me, "Go ahead, do your thing, sister, okay?" And I was feeling that I couldn't work under those conditions. What I needed to do was help them to find their way back to themselves.

One of the exercises I gave them was to be with each other overnight and not talk about any work. It was hard, but with careful monitoring, they were able to do it. People found themselves telling jokes, putting makeup on one another, and just relaxing and letting that warrior thing go. As a result of the work that was done at that retreat, they were able to find one another. They realized that everybody needed to take breaks from the struggle, and that it would still be there when they came back. Moreover, taking breaks in itself requires planning with others so the work keeps going on while that individuals take needed time off.

Another key lesson learned on this same retreat was the importance of learning how to sustain our work over the long haul. The people in the retreat saw that they were all doing wonderful things, but realized that they needed to learn how to do their work more strategically. This included doing the work from their own cultural centers and with accountability to one another.

—Circie Olatunji, New Orleans Coordinator

For people of color, staying centered (or staying in our "right minds") begins where we are naturally located and where we make up the critical mass—our kitchen tables, our churches, our community organizations. In these settings we can be accountable to and supported by our own communities. When we are in settings outside of our own communities, we can use the strength of knowing who we are and our connections to our own communities to meet the challenges we face—for example, being isolated or getting labeled as the conscience, the moral thermometer, or the radical of the groups with which we work.

People of color working in multiethnic environments need to create ties with other people from our communities of color and talk together about how to ensure that the needs or agenda of our communities are in the center rather than on the periphery of discussions. We need to consider questions such as, What does a suggested course of action mean from a religious, economic, or political perspective? What am I really accomplishing here for my community? What are we accomplishing for our community? When we ask these questions in connection with people from our communities, we can collectively move the center of multiethnic groups' discourse and agenda.

When we are being authentic, being real, we also create a process for being accountable to one another and our specific communities. If we don't do this, we run the risk of buying into someone else's agenda. We sometimes are so concerned about speaking the jargon and generally surviving in systems that are outside of who we are or where we come from that we carry our "survival" behaviors into our home environments. People in our own communities and homes start looking at us like, "Who are you?" The whole thing gets us confused and mixed up. We can help each other become conscious of and avoid falling into these traps. We don't have to unwittingly or unwillingly go into default mode. We can stay who we are and insist on our agenda becoming an equal part of our work in multiethnic groups. If we do this vigilantly, then we can function in healthy ways and create the outcomes that we want. We must become uncompromising in the knowledge that our communities are life affirming, and we must create ways to act out of that knowledge.

Looking Forward

Our voices are now clearer and stronger as women of color working on culturally relevant anti-bias approaches in early childhood education. We now know that we want to do more work that focuses specifically on culturally appropriate practice. We're clear about needing to understand the ways in which children are damaged by racism and other forms of oppression. We know that we need to make that information available to parents. We are becoming more adept at training adults in communities of color. We're clearer about the need to develop support mechanisms for people of color who are trying to implement culturally relevant practices in predominately white early childhood institutions and organizations, and we are beginning to devise ways to do that. And we're clear that anti-bias work must be conducted in culturally relevant ways consistent with the world views of the community with whom we are working. Consequently our work will look different, depending on the cultures of the children, families, and communities with whom we are working.

From our perspective, culturally relevant anti-bias educational approaches address the whole learning community (children, families, educators, administrators, artists, and so forth), are culturally based, and center around undoing oppression and supporting humanity.

And, ultimately, all this says is that there is no one recipe for doing culturally relevant anti-bias educational work. We each have to make it appropriate for the children and families in our centers and classrooms. Culture is dynamic. That is why there is a range of diversity even within the same ethnic group and points of tension and conflict that require respectful and fair negotiations. Furthermore, each of us brings multiple aspects of our personal identity to our interchanges with others. From mother, student, administrator, and parent to individual, neighbor, driver,

participant, and speaker—all of the various aspects of ourselves take the foreground or background even in the course of one conversation. We have to be flexible and respectful enough to allow other people to be where they are. We have to know when to get out of their way (or how to get them out of our way) when they are destructive to our children, our communities, and to themselves. All of these factors must affect our approaches to culturally relevant anti-bias educational work in each setting where we are attempting to implement it.

In Closing

Borrowing from the title of Myles Horton and Paulo Freire's book, we did indeed "make the road by walking." Such a project had never been done quite like this one before. We saw great value in bringing together people from different backgrounds (cultural, ethnic, economic, gender, sexual preference, religious, and so on). It really was a place to practice cross-cultural and cross-issue collaboration and discussion. As people of color, we learned that there are skills and strategies that our people need to learn in order to be effective and productive in these mixed settings. We also recognize that this project it is not the only way for people of color to organize around issues of oppression for young children and their families. There are times within the context of a CRAB group and within the context of an ethnic-specific group when we will need to meet separately and discuss issues, needs, and skills that are specific to ourselves. We hope these discussions have been reflected in this chapter.

Finally, we would like to recognize how our learnings relate to the work of Antonia Darder and her cultural response patterns for people of color. In *Culture and Power in the Classroom* she identifies four primary ways that bicultural people or people of color in the United States respond to racial oppression: (1) alienating yourself from your cultural group and aligning as much as possible with the dominant culture; (2) living a dual life culturally, so that at work or school you are like the dominant culture and at home you are like your home culture; (3) separating yourself as much as possible from the dominant culture and only relating with your own cultural group; and (4) negotiating a bicultural identity from a place

of power. We have discussed what parents might gain from these different response patterns. Antonia Darder believes that the fourth response of cultural negotiation is the one that holds the most hope for children of color and their families within the school system. Participating in a mixed cultural project such as the CRAB project provided us with ways to practice our cultural negotiation strategies, such as moving the center, avoiding the default mode, and including our languages and culturally based communication styles in the everyday functioning of the project and our work with one another. For that, in and of itself, it has been productive work.

Resources

Darder, Antonia. *Culture and Power in the Classroom: A Critical Foundation for Bicultural Education.* New York: Bergin, 1991.

Louise Derman-Sparks
Stacey York

Chapter 8

The European American Journey

Doing culturally relevant anti-bias education work is a lifetime journey—one of simultaneous personal growth, transformation of early childhood programs and community services, and community building. European Americans each come to this kind of work at different points. We have different life experiences. Some have had a great number of cross-cultural relationships. Others grew up in racially isolated communities and have very little experience with cross-cultural relationships. Some had parents who were involved in social justice work, and it seems to be in our blood. Others grew up with parents who might be described as bigots. Some grew up with the privileges of gender, race, class, and religion. Others grew up with various experiences of discrimination because we grew up poor, female, with a disability, or because we liked to do things beyond the gender-role expectations of our family or school. Each of us also comes to CRAB work with varying levels of self-awareness and acceptance of our multifaceted identities. Yet with all of this diversity among European Americans, a shared "white" experience still emerges when we grapple with our understanding of, place in, and responsibility for social change around the issue of racism.

In this chapter the two of us discuss our own particular journeys toward anti-racism in the context of the CRAB project. Both of us began work on racism and other types of oppression before the CRAB project, and we have continued it since the project ended. While our experiences

are reflective of the experiences of the European American CRAB participants, they are of course individual as well. (For further discussion of the
stages of European American development toward anti-racist consciousness and behavior, see Derman-Sparks and Phillips' *Teaching/ Learning
Anti-Racism;* Helms' *Black and White Racial Identity,* Tatum's "Teaching
White Students About Racism," and Thompson and Tyagi's *Names We
Call Home*). While we do not assume that every European American's
experience is like ours, we hope our story will help you uncover, illu-
minate, and clarify your own pathways toward greater liberation and
healing from the damage racism does to us and has taught us to do to
others.

Coming Face to Face with Racism and Removing the Blinders

Coming into a deep understanding of racism as an institutional, historic force as well as an interpersonal dynamic was at once the catalyst
for change and a continuing challenge for both of us. It is not possible
to reach this understanding in a moment, in a flash of enlightenment. It
takes many years and experiences to begin to untangle the many ways in
which institutional racism shapes our society and our experiences. For
each of us, however, there was a moment when we recognized the
endemic nature of racism in American society. There were also defining
points along the way when we experienced a lifting of the intellectual
and emotional blinders that prevented us from seeing societal racism,
when we said, "Aha, I get it!"

> **Stacey:** For me, it was as if I had woken from a deep sleep, from the
> protected environment of my growing up years in a comfortable,
> middle-class, mainly white environment. I particularly remember
> feeling overwhelmed. Suddenly racism seemed so big, so all-
> encompassing. I felt so stupid, so naive, as if I had been duped. I
> blamed myself for not having "gotten" racism. I realize that white
> people like me are incredibly protected and shielded from the reali-
> ties of racism. But I had expected more from myself.
>
> **Louise:** For me, the "Aha" about institutional racism felt like

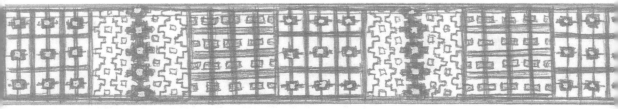

plunging from the surface of the problem to its deep, whirling core. Having grown up in a Jewish, working-class activist family, and having lived for several years in a low-income housing project, I knew that social injustice existed. As a child I was taught that the way to overcome racial prejudice was being "colorblind," and I frequently felt guilty because I noticed differences among the multiethnic population of New York City. Deeper understanding of the dynamics of systemic or institutional racism and the role of white people in their creation and perpetuation was at once comforting, because it confirmed my own perceptions, and overwhelming.

Beginning to understand racism as systemic helped me to make better sense of the world, and to realize that being colorblind was not the solution (or even desirable, because that perspective negated people's differing cultural and social realities). At the same time, I was overwhelmed by the realization that, strive as I might to reject prejudiced beliefs and behaviors, I still benefited and would always benefit from my position as a "white" person in a racist system. For many years I reacted to this understanding with serious "white guilt." Moreover, I had to face the fact that my commitment to eliminating racism was to be lifelong and all encompassing.

Many of the other European American CRAB participants also reported key moments of grasping the systemic nature of racism and white people's privileged position within it. Participants talked about how they thought they had understood racism for the past twenty years and had considered themselves anti-racists. And now, as a result of the CRAB experience, they realized that, while thinking they were working to eliminate racism, they in fact hadn't fully understood it and had even participated in its perpetuation.

Some of the feelings triggered by coming face to face with the realities of institutional racism resulted in behaviors that initially undercut our ability to be effective in working with other European Americans.

Stacey: When I look back, I see that some of the anti-racism training I experienced involved a lot of good information, but it didn't provide any opportunity for me to process my feelings. I realize now that this was too assaulting for me. What happened to me next I've

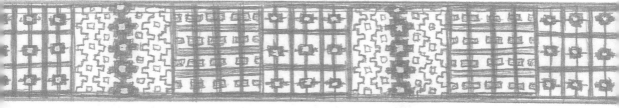

seen happen to lots of other European Americans. For a period of time I became a "hell and damnation" anti-racism trainer. In a period of about two years, I went from being afraid to use the "R-word" (racism) in trainings for fear of offending white people, to telling all white people that they were racists and that they needed to do something about it, and *now.* I was feeling incompetent, inadequate, vulnerable, and exposed, so I ended up making other people feel the same way.

Louise: In my early days as a trainer, I felt guilty, so I thought I had accomplished my purpose of teaching other white people how deeply we were all enmeshed in the system of racism and our primary responsibility for ending it if they also felt guilty. I also thought guilt would motivate people to get more active. I eventually realized that my version of the "hell and damnation" approach tended to immobilize people or result in their taking inappropriate actions.

Now, in retrospect, and with greater understanding of the European American journey, we believe our desire to do "hell and damnation" training with other whites is a stage, coming soon after the initial breakthrough "Aha" of facing racism. We saw this stage of the journey in several of the European American participants in the CRAB project. (Of course, as with any other general pattern of behavior, not all anti-racist white people do this.) But as we reflect on the CRAB experience, we have come to the conclusion that we would like to lessen the impact of the "hell and damnation" stage of interacting with other European Americans, and we can do even more in the future to structure our training so people can productively deal with the feelings triggered by the discovery of the nature of racism and their role in it. This especially means paying careful attention to issues of European American cultural identity and our social-political location in institutional racism.

Stacey: Another common trap that I and some of the other European Americans in the CRAB groups fell into was the fear of making a mistake in front of other European Americans. White people doing anti-racism work can become so competitive with one another. It's like a contest to see who can be the best anti-racist white person. The idea is that there are good white people and bad white people, and the bad white people don't "get it." And we all want to be seen as a good white person. All of our participants were respected leaders in the early childhood community. Who wants to fall flat on her face in front of her professional peers? Who wants to look or sound racist in front of her peers? I was afraid of making a mistake in front of the group, and the group members were afraid to make mistakes in front of me and one another. We constantly had our defenses up. Again, this situation points to the need for a more proactive process to help European Americans face all of our fears and insecurities.

A Cultural Identity of One's Own

For several years both of us got stuck believing that being white was the single most defining part of ourselves. Being white became not just a life reality but also a life sentence. Cirecie Olatunji, Sharon Henry, and Sharon Cronin helped us both see that culture, not "race," is the key to our identity. We have come to understand, as a result of the CRAB part of our journey, that our "whiteness" has to do with our sociopolitical location in the system of racism but is not what defines us as human beings.

On the one hand, that position does give us white privilege, and we both have experienced much guilt and shame over what white people have done to people of color in North America in the past five hundred years. On the other hand, our location in racism is not the same as our cultural identity—it does not make us who we are as whole people. Reaffirming and embracing culture brought us healing, albeit through somewhat different paths.

> **Stacey:** My first step was to reclaim myself as a cultural being. This wasn't easy at first, because I had never really thought about myself as a cultural being, only as an individual person in a particular family. Changing that involved making a conscious effort to identify myself as a European American rather than a white person. It involved recognizing how my culture has shaped my thinking, the way I process information, my communication style, and the way I express feelings. Accepting myself as a

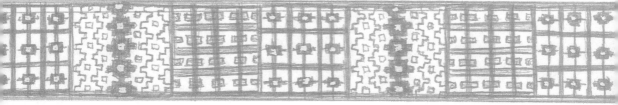

European American and acknowledging the ways in which I, in fact, behave like a European American helped me begin to see that being white is not all bad. I like my linear style of thinking. I value clear, direct communication. Learning about my culture and embracing my home culture helped me feel more self-accepting.

As is often the case, self-acceptance leads to acceptance of others. Affirming my cultural identity helped me reconnect to other European Americans. While I was working on this book, my family circumstances dictated that we move from an integrated urban neighborhood to a predominantly European American suburb. Now it's much easier for me to be with my own people and to accept my own people. I am able to challenge them in gentler, more respectful, and ultimately more effective ways.

Recently I had a wonderful experience reconnecting with my Dutch roots. My husband surprised me with a weekend trip to Pella, Iowa, to celebrate tulip time. It was so much fun to be around so many other Dutch people. It amazed me how much we all looked alike. A friend loaned me a traditional Dutch dress and I wore it with a new pair of wooden shoes in the parade through town. I hadn't worn a traditional Dutch outfit since I was a child. I had worn wooden shoes off and on throughout childhood, so they felt very comforting. My husband also dressed in traditional Dutch clothing and walked with me, our friends, and my goddaughter. We looked just like the picture of my great grandparents that hung in my grandparents' bedroom. I experienced the deep peace that comes from knowing who you are and where you come from.

Louise: My shift in how I view my identity was strongly influenced by my connecting with other white people doing anti-racism work and by rethinking how I feel about my Jewish identity. These important steps in my personal journey did not happen alone. They were sparked by my experiences at the New Orleans based People's Institute for Survival and Beyond, and by my relationship with Cecelia Alvarado and Phyllis Brady through our work as trainers in the California AEYC's Leadership-in-Diversity program. Working with Sharon Cronin, Sharon Henry, Cirecie Olatunji, and Stacey York continued the process.

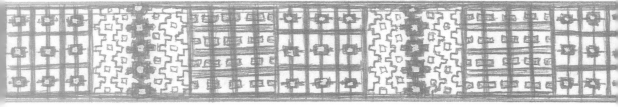

Getting to know and having numerous discussions with other European American anti-racist activists at a national training retreat of the People's Institute for Survival and Beyond was a transforming experience. That was the first time that I had really spent serious time with a group of white anti-racists. Being with people who were struggling with issues similar to mine, who affirmed me as a person, and who supported my work while also collectively acknowledging our sociopolitical location within racism was wonderfully healing. I realized that I had put an unnecessary burden on myself by letting my "white guilt" prevent me from feeling all right about who I was. I decided I was going to stop doing this to myself and instead accept myself for who I am, with all of the contradictions involved in being a white person in the struggle against racism.

The second part of my finding a cultural identity of my own resulted from being pushed to rethink what being Jewish meant to me, especially in the context of doing culturally relevant anti-bias work. A cultural sharing activity at the People's Institute training started this shift for me. I was able to clearly state to myself and to the group my ambivalent feelings: I am very proud of my Jewish heritage and culture, but I am also angry about and ashamed of some of the current attitudes and behavior of many in my cultural group toward people of color in this country and toward the Palestinians in Israel. At the same time I realized I could embrace what was good in my cultural heritage while acknowledging what was oppressive. I didn't have to reject the whole package. This was my turning point. Then I could also acknowledge the realities of anti-Semitism in my life and the ways it has hurt me.

I am now much more comfortable about being imperfect and living with contradictions. I have become more authentic. I believe this has made me more effective in my work with others. I am also much less threatened when I get called on acting out of white privilege. I sleep better.

Staying in Our "Right Minds"

Both of us recognize that as long as systemic racism exists in our country we will always have to face the complexity of a cultural identity that

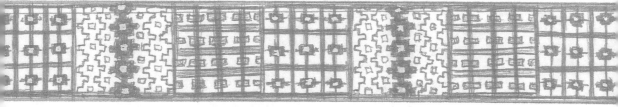

gives us wholeness and strength and the realities of our white privilege. Coming to terms with this truth and our complex feelings about it is a lifelong journey. Sometimes we have to push through the pain we feel about it to avoid getting stuck. It is definitely worth the effort because it has meant coming to a much clearer, stronger, and more peaceful sense of self and finding much more energy to effectively do our life's work.

Calling ourselves "European American" does not remove these complexities, but it does remind us that white people do have cultural selves that shape and give meaning to who we are in the world—cultural identities that originate in the ethnic groups and geographic places from which our families first came, and that were further shaped on the anvil of our groups' history in the United States. Acknowledging this reality is central to our healing from the damage racism has done to us, although we also have to be careful of the potential for using our ethnic and cultural histories as a way to avoid the power issues involved in being white.

To explore the relationship between our European American cultural identities and our position as "white" within the system of institutional racism, we have found it helpful to ask ourselves questions such as the following:

- What kind of power do I have as a European American to challenge the status quo and initiate change?
- What are my particular roles and contributions to integrating culturally relevant anti-bias approaches into early childhood care and education?
- How effectively am I carrying out the roles? Where am I slipping into racist power behaviors?

Some of the European Americans in the CRAB groups in Seattle and Minneapolis/St. Paul formed "European Dissent" groups, inspired by the people in the New Orleans CRAB group who had organized such a group several years ago. These groups have been incredibly important for helping European Americans stay in our "right minds" (paying attention to the multidimensional relation between our sociopolitical location in racism and our cultural identity). The groups provide an ongoing way to keep learning, to analyze what it takes to work in various European American communities, to give (and get) emotional and tactical support, and to keep each other accountable through critical feedback. It is very important to make sure that people in groups like this are also working with and getting feedback from people of color doing culturally relevant anti-bias and anti-racism work. Otherwise, we run the danger of falling into the traps of white privilege and supremacist thinking.

Relationships with other European Americans

Deconstructing racism, recovering our cultural identities, and understanding our role as white people in eliminating racism also made it possible to have more effective relationships with other white people as we did our CRAB work. Our goal was to become more able to temper our newfound awareness, anger, and energy for change with compassion and staying connected to the people with whom we were working.

In the process of achieving these behaviors the two of us and other CRAB members grappled with the ongoing pain and weariness of feeling "different" from other white people. We had to break one of the key rules of European American society—not to confront one another about racism. We had to learn how not to personalize hostility from other European Americans who disagreed with us, and how not to fall into the protective stance of "I'm the *good* white person." We sometimes face a "heart thumping wildly" reaction when we realize we have to say something to interrupt the racism of others and try to do it in a way that is constructive rather than only angry.

> **Stacey:** This was the most difficult aspect for me. I can remember times when other European Americans complained that I was too hard on them. I really respect those that can go through this journey and not lose their connection to their own people. I lost my connection and have begun to reclaim it.
>
> There are many times when I am with other European Americans and I am the only one to see the racism inherent in a situation, or my view on a particular topic is totally different from everyone else's. I remember being at a neighborhood Christmas

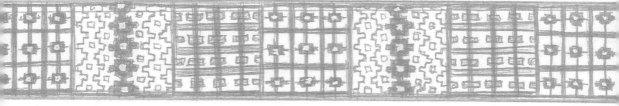

party last year where the topic of Ebonics came up. People were going off right and left, mocking the notion that there could be Black English and bemoaning the use of their tax dollars to teach people how to speak another language. Their understanding of the issue was limited to what they had read in the newspaper and what they had heard on AM talk radio. I tried to broaden the discussion by relating what I know about Ebonics and my views. They thought I was nuts, and they clearly did not appreciate having me break ranks and weaken their white solidarity. Initially these kinds of situations make me mad. But later I feel sad, isolated, and begin to entertain self-doubt. I start wondering to myself, "Am I the crazy one? Why is it that I see this stuff and others don't?" And I need to have European American colleagues and friends that I can go to who can help me process situations and affirm that I am not crazy.

I have one very fond memory of an evening at an anti-racism training. Four of us European Americans were sitting around in our room at the retreat center drinking wine and talking about all kinds of things. We talked about our feelings, our families, and ourselves as people. We laughed and laughed. It was really fun, but most importantly I experienced the acceptance of a group of gentle European Americans, each of whom had committed their lives to anti-racism work and who, at the same time, knew how to laugh and have a good time. And they didn't need to put anybody down in order to build themselves up.

Louise: I feel much more at peace with myself since I have connected to other anti-racist European Americans—CRAB members, others throughout the United States, and anti-racist white people around the world. It is a very caring community to whom I can go for help—be it information, ideas, critiques, or emotional support—without fearing to show my limitations. This kind of dependable support also frees me to work more compassionately and effectively with other European Americans. My own journey gives me personal evidence that accepting who I am frees me to do this work.

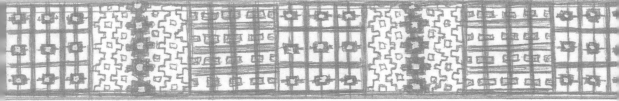

Accepting, Understanding, and Appreciating Our Role as European Americans in the Struggle Against Racism and Other Systemic Oppression

Stacey: Writing *Roots and Wings* back in the late 1980s brought me to a crisis point. About halfway through, I stopped writing. I thought to myself, "What do I have to say about multicultural education? Who do I think I am—that I have something to say and people should listen to me? It's only my white privilege that would ever have allowed me to think that I could be a spokesperson on the topic of diversity." Now I realize that I was falling into the trap of thinking that European Americans don't have or can't have anything to say, that only people of color have a legitimate right to be leaders in the work to end racism. Of course, this type of thinking perpetuates the practice of keeping people of color responsible for racism and keeps European Americans off the hook.

Louise: Early on in my journey I came to believe deeply that white people carry the primary responsibility for ending racism, because it is white people who created it in this country and on this continent. Consequently I also see European Americans' primary work as being with other European Americans. However, I struggle with the critical issue of the different roles and relationships of European Americans and people of color who are doing culturally relevant anti-bias education work. At the core of this relationship is the nature of accountability to people of color. The question is how to develop goals and strategies that interrupt and change racism's power dynamics and to catch ourselves when the work we do plays into these power dynamics.

Another key ongoing aspect of my journey is to understand more deeply how the interconnections between racism and other systemic oppressions based on class, gender, and sexual orientation affect working with other European Americans. Our discussions in the CRAB groups clearly highlighted the complexity and difficulties of these issues within a multiethnic group. They pushed all of us to stretch, as well as pushing our various sore points.

I learned through the CRAB experience, as we all did, that answers to both of these questions can only come through building on-

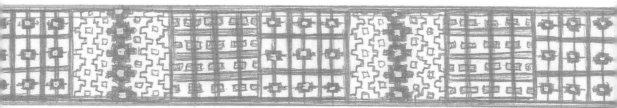

Knowing the Costs and Benefits of Anti-Racism Work

The following list of costs and benefits contributed by the European American members of the Minneapolis/St. Paul group is similar to those compiled by the European American members of the Seattle and New Orleans groups. This activity helped us understand how our personal experiences and feelings stem from systemic racism, not from personal inadequacies.

Costs:

- Feeling lonely/alienated from other white people (family, friends, and coworkers) because you see things they don't see;
- Having people put you in a box or label you (for example, "That's just Stacey. She's really into that trip.") as a way of dismissing what you have to say;
- Sadness/grief;
- Jealousy/competition with other anti-racist white people;
- Having to face oneself and one's family history;
- Loss of ignorance, and consequently feeling that nothing is simple anymore;
- Having to admit one's ignorance;
- Loss of job or loss of a promotion; fewer job options; getting marginalized within one's field;
- Experiencing the difficult physical, mental, and emotional labor of culturally relevant anti-bias work;
- Living with the fact that white privilege lets us walk away from this work at any time; knowing at the same time that if we do that we lose our integrity and peace of mind; and
- Questioning whether we as white people have a right to do this work.

Benefits

- Gaining a sense of hope that comes from taking action;
- Gaining a sense of integrity from being honest;
- Attaining wholeness (bring my spirituality, beliefs, creativity to one's work) and healing/psychological health;
- Gaining conflict resolution and management skills; learning not to fear or avoid conflict;
- Moving away from dualistic either/or thinking; opening up to new possibilities;
- Enjoying inner satisfaction of doing justice work;
- Enjoying freedom from ideological myths;
- Gaining a new sense of European American culture/ethnic identity;
- Learning how to take care of oneself;
- Learning to read the world more accurately;
- Learning about and from white people who have opposed and worked to end racism;
- Having closer authentic relationships with people of color; and
- Working for the survival of our country.

going, honest, frank discussions and working relationships with one another and from the reflections we do about our work in our various communities.

Changing Our Power Dynamics with People of Color

Deconstructing racism, taking responsibility to work to end it, and finding ourselves as cultural beings make it possible to have authentic cross-cultural relationships. As European Americans we have to have something to bring to a relationship. We can't just remain ignorant and expect people of color to "teach" us about racism and how to behave. When we work on ourselves, we can begin to monitor ourselves by

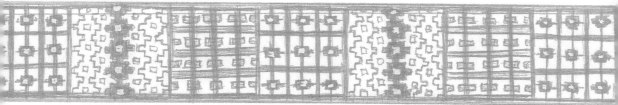

asking questions such as Do I share time in conversations? Do I always have to have the last word? Do I interrupt in midsentence or try to tell a person of color what I think she is trying to say? Am I able to acknowledge my mistakes, say I'm sorry, and work on not repeating them? Do I respect the boundaries of our relationship?

We both really try to be allies. What that means is recognizing and naming racism when it occurs and calling other European Americans on their racism. It means offering support and encouragement and using our institutional power whenever possible to further the agenda of communities of color. It means facing the fact that the cross-cultural power dynamics created by racism are reproduced again and again, even when we are working our hardest not to do so. And it means nondefensively accepting criticism and changing specific behaviors.

The CRAB groups gave us the unusual opportunity to be in a multi-ethnic group of people hearing and struggling with one another's perspectives, pushing each other's personal growth, and honestly trying to learn. We got past the being polite stage to the messy stage and grew from it, albeit sometimes kicking and screaming at first. For example, through the discussions with the other authors of this book, the two of us got clearer about the concept of "moving the center" and how we have to back off sometimes so the shift can happen. We confessed to each other that, while we completely agreed, we both also had anxious feelings (Do I still have a role? What will it be? Will I like it? What am I supposed to do?). There are no easy answers or assurances. We realize that we can only find the answers by living the questions.

We had to let go of our fear that when we make mistakes we will be seen as racist, and that will end our relationships with people of color in the group. We all struggled to persevere. For example, during the writing of this book there were several occasions among the five of us when we said, "I'm not ever going to talk to that person again!" Yet we kept coming back, because we need one another on the journey toward the vision we share.

Finally, one of the unexpected lessons we both learned about ourselves is how we were equating being serious about this work with never having fun. Cirecie Olatunji, Sharon Henry, and Sharon Cronin taught us how to play while doing serious work. We have to take time to dance,

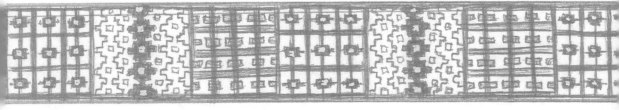

to eat good meals, to connect on a personal level, to go window shopping, and to laugh. We did some of our best thinking together during or immediately after a fun afternoon.

Understanding the Rhythm of Our Growth and Hanging in for the Long Haul

At different times over the past five years we found ourselves needing to reaffirm our commitment to this work and to each other. As in other journeys, we experienced peaks and valleys, detours, rest stops, periods of rapid movement, and periods of slow motion. Each of us attempted to maintain a balance between our personal and professional lives and our commitment to the CRAB group and work.

> **Stacey:** I can remember different times in the journey when I was going through rapid periods of growth and just couldn't let in another new idea or work on another behavior. There were other times when one or another CRAB participant had to step back and let others carry the load. Babies, parents dying, going back to school, illness, surgery, and other family crises called us away from time to time. We needed to recognize that pulling back to attend to our families doesn't mean we are not committed to one another or this work. A collaborative, trusting group allows its members to have their time away while the work keeps going. Knowing that doing culturally relevant anti-bias work is going to be a lifelong process reminds us to sustain ourselves for the long haul.

The steps and rhythms of our own journeys are a powerful source for understanding what other European Americans go through. Our growth keeps us believing in the possibilities of growth and change in others. The journey we took together as the two European American leaders in the CRAB leadership team greatly deepened our relationship as we turned to each other for help and support. We know our long journey to understand and change institutional racism is worth all the pain and uncertainty we have experienced, because by taking it we truly reclaim our humanity and participate in the long and honorable struggle to create a world in which everyone is able to be fully human.

Resources

Derman-Sparks, Louise, and Carol Brunson Phillips. *Teaching/Learning Anti-Racism: A Developmental Approach*. New York: Teachers College Press, 1997.

Helms, Janet, ed. *Black and White Racial Identity: Theory, Research, and Practice.* Westport, CT: Greenwood, 1990.

Tatum, Beverly Daniel. "Teaching White Students about Racism: The Search for White Allies and the Restoration of Hope." Teachers College Record 95 (4).

Thompson, Becky, and Sangeeta Tyagi. *Names We Call Home: Autobiography on Racial Identity.* New York: Routledge, 1996.

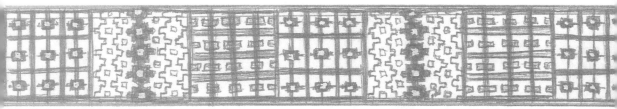

Louise Derman-Sparks
Sharon Cronin
Sharon Henry
Cirecie Olatunji
Stacey York

 Guidelines for Setting Up an Early Childhood Activist Group in Your Community

Strategic thinking requires a willingness to consider all alternatives, to share the information needed to develop them, and to commit to following through on a plan of action that best serves the long-term interests of the whole community.

—Tatanka Yotanka (Sitting Bull)

If you, like us, want to work toward cultural democracy and social justice in programs and services for children and families—in short, if you want to be an activist in your early childhood community—this chapter is for you. It offers guidelines for forming a group in your community that will have the capacity to provide the training, networking, and support necessary to take effective action. Our suggestions reflect what worked for us in forming the CRAB groups and also what we would do now, based on our reflections about our experiences. They will help you think through with others how to form a group that makes the most sense for your community's needs and realities.

GUIDELINE 1: Consider Your Own Strengths and Limitations for Initiating a Planning Process

There is a place for everyone in cultural democracy and social justice work, but it takes more than good intentions to be effective. We must be self-aware about who we are in relation to the systemic power dynamics in our society. We must assess the strengths and limitations we bring to the task. The following activities will help you do such a self-assessment and to identify others that you may need to work with to enhance your effectiveness. You may find it helpful to write down your responses or talk them over with a friend or colleague who shares your interests.

1. What is my social identity portrait?

Create your portrait:
Divide a piece of paper into two columns. In one column make a list of all the various groups that define your social identity. This list includes, at a minimum, your gender, class, race, ethnicity, culture, sexual orientation, and physical ability or disability. In the other column, across from each aspect of your social identity, indicate whether or not you receive general societal privilege in that category. For example, in the gender category, men as a group receive privilege over women. In the race category, whites as a group receive privilege over people of color.

Consider your position in relation to the various groups with which you work that make up your larger community:
For example, if your social identity primarily gives you societal privilege, you are more likely to have easier access to people in leadership and power within the early childhood education system and in funding agencies. On the other hand, your intentions may not be trusted by people in groups that do not receive societal privilege. This is not a commentary on your personal trustworthiness but rather a reflection of the "long shadow" cast by several hundred years of racism and other kinds of institutional oppression in our society. If your social identity primarily means that you do not receive societal privilege, you are likelier to have easier access within your own communities, but may have

fewer routes for getting access to funding or to people in power within the early childhood system. In all cases, our identities give us more possibilities in some areas and pose limitations in other areas.

2. Do I have a track record of experiences with various communities?

Examine your connections:

Make a list of the various groups that make up your community. Divide the list into the groups with which you have personal or professional connections and those with which you are not connected. Then ask yourself questions like the following to clarify the patterns in your list:

- ◆ What kinds of diversity are reflected in these communities?
- ◆ What kinds of connections do you have with people in each community? Are you primarily in the role of an observer (for example, attending occasional meetings that bring people together from different groups), or a helper (for example, going into a community to bring food or clothing)? Are you primarily in a social or work role? Do you socialize, attend a place of worship together, belong to a chorus or theater group? Do you work together in advocacy or political groups?
- ◆ If you are in a working relationship, are you functioning as a peer or holding a supervisory position?

Consider the power issues reflected in these connections and the way in which they affect both your knowledge of a particular community and the way in which people from that community may perceive you:

For example, if you are not a person of color, but you have strong peer connections with people of color, you will be in a better position to know or get information about the key people of color to involve in the planning process and what kinds of advocacy work is already going on in communities of color. However, if you have primarily been in an observer or helping role in communities of color, you are likelier to not yet have sufficient knowledge or relationships of trust to ask people to work with you on creating an activist group.

Given these constraints, ask yourself with whom you might need to work to initiate a multiethnic, cross-cultural planning process; make a list of these people or communities.

3. Do I have a track record of cultural empowerment, diversity, and social justice work?

Make a list of all the ways you have been involved in this work:

Then ask yourself questions like the following to analyze your work:

- With what kinds of groups have you worked?
- What kinds of issues have you addressed (racism, sexism, classicism, ableism, heterosexism)?
- What issues were most important or powerful for you?
- Of the issues that are now present in your city or area, which ones have you not had experience with?
- With whom would you need to work to begin the process of setting up an activist group that would focus on multiple issues?

If this is your first attempt at working on diversity and social justice issues, then you are not ready to form an activist group on your own. You will need to seek out people who do have a track record and ask if they would be willing to work with and guide you.

4. Do I have a track record of working within the early childhood community?

Examine your connections to the early childhood community:

Your role within the early childhood community will also affect how open people will be to joining or supporting your effort to start an activist group. Record or discuss your answers to questions like the following:

- With what arenas of early childhood education and care do you have ties?
- Are you seen as a newcomer or an elder?
- Have you been active in early childhood professional organizations? If yes, which ones? If not, do you consider yourself, or are you seen as, an outsider?

Consider the effect your position within the early childhood community will have on your ability to be effective at starting an activist group:

It will probably be more difficult if you are perceived as a newcomer or outsider coming in to change what you have not been a part of. You may need to ask someone with more credentials who is also committed to social justice work to help you in the planning process. Conversely, if you are in a leadership position within the early childhood community, it is important to join with practitioners who bring the perspective of people at the "frontlines" of the work, as well as the perspective of those who have traditionally been outside of the power structure in early childhood.

5. Why do I want to do this? Am I prepared to stay with it?

Examine your reasons for wanting to do this work in this way:

If you choose to start an early childhood culturally relevant anti-bias group, you will be taking on a long-term, demanding piece of work that requires patience, hope, the ability to handle frustration, and persistence. Make a list of your reasons for wanting to do so.

In our experience, certain reasons underlie long-term staying power. These factors include choosing to do the work out of a sense of outrage of what oppression does to both yourself and others, holding a vision of how much better conditions could be for children and families, hoping that your vision will someday be realized, and accepting that the work will not take a neat, straight, or quick path. Reasons that do not make for long-term commitment include expecting short-term results and taking on the work primarily to enhance one's professional image or to change others.

6. Am I the best person to initiate the planning process of starting an early childhood activist group? With whom do I need to work to balance my strengths and limitations?

Self-aware and honest consideration of all of the preceding questions will enable you to then dispassionately consider whom you must include in taking the next steps. Thinking about these questions is an exercise in weighing your identity, experience, and connections against the diversity

in your community. It will be different for everyone who undertakes it. Following are two hypothetical scenarios to demonstrate how this process might work.

Anne is thinking about starting a cross-cultural group to address needs for culturally relevant anti-bias education in her area. She has identified these aspects of her identity and situation:

- a Latina woman;
- middle-class background;
- lives and works within the Latino community;
- lesbian;
- able-bodied (doesn't have a disability);
- active in early childhood organizations; and
- experienced in working in coalition with other groups on issues of nutrition and health care for poor children in her city.

Anne is in a position to identify other early childhood practitioners and parents within her Latino community who might be interested in an activist group. She has connections with advocacy groups and people of other ethnic backgrounds within the early childhood community who might join her in the planning process. She has connections with the gay and lesbian community as well, where there might also be parents and community members who would be interested in an activist group. She may need to think about how to bring in the voices of people from poor and working class backgrounds, as well those of people with disabilities.

Celeste also has been thinking about starting an activist group in her area. Her identity and experience profile look like this:

- a white woman;
- working-class background;
- lives in a white neighborhood;
- able-bodied (doesn't have a disability);
- works in a diverse child care center;
- a newcomer to early childhood education;

- hasn't been active in early childhood organizations; and
- active in women's movement activities.

Celeste will need to contact and work with a small group of other early childhood practitioners who have experience in early childhood work and doing social justice work around racism. She will also need to work with people who are active in professional early childhood organizations, people of color, and people who live and work in communities of color.

7. Based on your self-assessment, invite a few people to help you with the next two planning steps. Choose individuals whose experiences provide additional perspectives and knowledge beyond your own.

GUIDELINE 2: Prepare the Ground in Your Community

To form an early childhood activist group to address issues of oppression and cultural empowerment you will need to explore the issues, possibilities, and interest in forming a group with key people in the early childhood community, various cultural communities, and in social justice advocacy groups.

1. Create a diversity map of your city, community, or rural area.
Many of us have assumptions about the diversity in our communities or neighborhoods that turn out to be incomplete or incorrect after a more objective assessment. To counter this, investigate subcommunities with which you don't have personal experience. Take it as a given that your community is not homogeneous in some important ways and commit yourself to finding those ways.

Make a list of all of the kinds of diversity that exist in your area, with help from the few individuals you have asked to join you in these initial planning steps:
Sometimes in an apparently racially homogeneous community there are different ethnic or cultural groups. For example, in Vermont, a majority white state, 30 percent of the population is of French Canadian background. This cultural group has experienced oppression for at least a

century because of its language, culture, and class. In a city or area with a large Latino population, there may be several cultural differences related to people's nationality (Salvadoran, Mexican, Nicaraguan, Puerto Rican, and so on). The Deaf community has its own language (American Sign Language) and other cultural attributes, exists all over the United States, and is relatively invisible to hearing people. Also, take into account other kinds of diversity, and be sure to include people from a variety of class backgrounds, people from both urban and rural backgrounds where appropriate, people with disabilities, and people from the gay and lesbian community.

2. Create a diversity portrait of the early childhood system in your city and state.

Your ideas about the diversity in the early childhood system in your city and state may also be incomplete. To get a more compete picture, gather data on early childhood programs. Examine where children and families from different cultural and class backgrounds are located in early childhood programs by asking questions like those listed below. Use the answers to broaden the group of people with whom you are talking.

- What kinds of programs are available (family child care, center-based child care, Head Start, public or private preschool, programs for children with disabilities), and who uses which ones?
- Are families relatively segregated by class or culture?
- What are the staffing patterns in each type of program?
- Are child care workers segregated by culture or class? What about gender?
- What is the cultural, class, and gender mix of the people working in early childhood in your area, and how are they separated from each other?
- What is the leadership of early childhood programs, agencies, and organizations?
- How does that leadership break down by culture, class, and gender?

- What community advocacy organizations exist? Who is involved in those, both in terms of leadership and staffing? Are they diverse in terms of culture, gender, and class?

3. Make a list of individuals with whom you want to speak about the possibilities, issues, and needs for an early childhood activist group. Use the contacts you already have to help you formulate your initial list. Once you begin talking with people on your initial list, ask them for names of other individuals to contact. Include people in the following categories:

- people working in early childhood and other human service programs serving children and families from the various communities you listed in your diversity map. These will be a combination of early childhood workers you think may be committed to diversity and equity work, people in key programs such as your local resource and referral agency and community-specific based agencies, faculty at community colleges, and leaders in your local early childhood organizations;
- individuals who are considered elders and informal leaders in the various cultural communities in your city, community, or rural area. Talk to people running cultural, advocacy, and human service programs in these communities for ideas; and
- leaders and active members in advocacy groups concerned with children, families, and issues of oppression in the various ethnic and cultural communities in your city, community, or rural area, as well as groups with a citywide, statewide, or regional focus.

4. Begin the process of building relationships and ensuring buy-in from the essential players in your city.
Contact people and set up informal meetings. Let the people you are contacting choose the meeting place. Don't rush this step. Take time to get to know people, to understand their issues, and to build solid working relationships.

GUIDELINE 3: Form a Planning Committee

The planning committee sets the framework for establishing an activist group. It has the tasks of identifying the mission, goals, and general makeup of the activist group. The planning committee also decides on publicity and recruitment, selects of group participants and group coordinators, and makes plans for local fund-raising.

1. Keep the planning committee large enough to represent diverse viewpoints but small enough to be manageable. Ten to fifteen people is usually a good size. Be sure to include people from diverse backgrounds, including:

- individuals coming from the various cultural communities with which you wish to work;
- people representing other kinds of diversity (class, gender, religion, sexual preference, disability, and so forth);
- people from all levels of the early childhood field; and
- people with community organizing experience.

2. Consider starting with an initial meeting to which you invite all of the key people who are interested in helping to form an early childhood activist group.

Use this meeting to collectively identify and assess the reasons why an activist group focused on cultural and social justice issues in relation to young children and families is needed in your city or region. Identify a mission and long-term goals and identify the desired make-up of the group. Consider questions like the following: Will it be multiethnic? Will it reflect other forms of diversity? Will the group only or primarily include early childhood care and education practitioners, a mixture of parents and early childhood practitioners, or a more broadly based group of people, including community organizers who provide services to families?

If you choose to start with a more broadly based planning group, invite a larger group of people than you expect to need for the planning committee. Around twenty to twenty-five people is desirable. Ask a person in your community having experience as an organizational devel-

opment consultant to help you plan and facilitate this meeting. You may also find someone who is willing to donate her time from a local college or an existing community development organization.

When you start the process by meeting with this larger group, the planning committee can form in a variety of ways. The planning committee may come from the participants in the initial planning meeting. A few people from the initial meeting may take on the responsibility of selecting and inviting individuals to be on the planning committee. Or you may decide to work with a few of the people you met when collecting data and building contacts to decide on the people to invite to join the planning committee.

3. Pay attention to cultural dynamics from the beginning.

At your first meeting, set up a way of working together that takes into the account the various cultural needs of the planning group members and "moves the center" away from status quo dominance by European American culture. Expect that there will be conflicts and challenges in the planning process. Help one another understand where each conflict is coming from (for example, cultural differences, power issues, different community needs) and negotiate solutions. Consider the following factors in making the meeting culturally accessible.

Meeting location

Consider geographic location. What is comfortable to some individuals may not be comfortable to others. You may want to hold the meeting in various communities rather than in just one. Consider the building in which you will meet. A room in a local community center, a church, or a meeting space at one of the member's work sites will have different appeal to various members. Find out what people prefer. It is also important that the site be accessible to people with disabilities. Find out the accessibility needs of committee members and verify the site with them to be sure that it really is accessible to them. Also take into account the accessibility of the meeting site by public transportation.

Meeting time

Some committee members may not be able to meet during work hours. For example, people working directly with children are less likely to be able to get time off, whereas people in supervisory positions or higher education instructors will probably find it easier. If you meet in the evenings, consider the fact that some people may first need to get their children home from child care and feed them, and some may need to wake up very early the following morning.

Communication style and pacing

Some people jump right in as soon as another speaker pauses, and others believe a brief pause between speaking is a respectful way to proceed. Some people need time to process issues before speaking, and others think out loud. Some individuals speak up as soon as the discussion begins and others wait, particularly when speaking with their elders or leaders. Always check in to make sure that all participants have a chance to say what they want and agree on ways to ensure equitable speaking time for all committee members.

Power dynamics

Remember that even though all the planning committee members are committed to working on cultural and social justice issues, all of us have been socialized within a racist, sexist, and otherwise oppressive society. We act out the dynamics of institutionalized power even when we do not want to or are unaware that we are so doing. A planning group facilitator who is aware of these dynamics and knows how to help people become conscious of them will enable the planning committee to function productively. This person can pay informed attention to who is talking, who is being silent, and whose interests are on the agenda.

The committee may also want to participate in some anti-racism or anti-oppression training so that all of its members grow in their self-awareness and understanding of internalized privilege and oppression.

Child care during meetings

Availability of on-site child care will make it possible for some people to attend who would otherwise not be able to do so. The location you choose for the meeting will be affected by the need for child care arrangements. A related issue is providing coverage for child care providers if the meeting is scheduled during the day. In centers, coverage can often be arranged, but family home providers often need help finding and paying for someone to provide child care in their places if meetings are held during the day.

Food and drink

Remember that many people have dietary restrictions. In addition, almost everyone has preferences. For example, some people only eat "healthy food" while others prefer more "popular culture" snacks and drinks.

Translation and interpretation

It may be necessary to rent simultaneous translation equipment if two or more languages are spoken by people on the planning committee. If Deaf people are involved in planning, a sign language interpreter will have to be provided.

GUIDELINE 4: Carrying Out the Planning Committee's Tasks

1. Assess the needs for an early childhood activist group focused on cultural and social justice in your city or region, including a comprehensive look at the diversity map of your city or region and the diversity demographics in the early childhood system. (If you held an initial larger meeting, then the planning committee can build on its discussion.)

2. Identify an initial mission and long-term goals for the activist group. Once the activist group forms, it will develop these further.

3. Identify the desired makeup of the group. Will it be multiethnic? Will it reflect other forms of diversity? Will the group only or primarily include early childhood care and education practitioners, have a mixture

of parents and early childhood practitioners, or include community activists concerned with providing relevant, culturally empowering services to children and families?

4. Consider the group's relationship to existing agencies and organizations. There are pros and cons to being either independent or connected to an already established group. In general, being structurally independent of existing groups is advantageous since the group's purpose is to address existing inequities and unmet needs and to create change within the early childhood system and other existing services to children and families. However, some current groups are being supported by their state or local AEYC affiliate. In these cases advantages include the existence of a source for funding and administrative support, as well as built-in ties to the early childhood community.

5. Develop a plan for publicity and recruitment that will appeal to and reach various communities. Remember that insufficiently diverse recruiting methods can result in mistakes that are not easily forgotten or forgiven (for example, leaving out a key cultural community in your planning can lead to not getting the kind of applicant pool you want). Make sure all of your public relations and recruitment efforts reach early childhood practitioners as well as program directors, agency heads, and members of community groups, as well as their leaders.

Recruit proactively by talking to individual people face to face or over the phone. Ask for a few moments to speak to people at community group meetings, advocacy group meetings, or early childhood staff meetings. Conduct presentations at various organizations and agencies. Ask local early childhood and advocacy groups focused on children and families to send flyers to everyone on their mailing lists. Send out written flyers in all the languages spoken by the people in your city, community, or rural area. Write an article in your local early childhood newsletter.

To build interest in an activist group that will organize around issues of cultural democracy and social justice in the early childhood community, you may want to present workshops about cultural relevancy and

anti-bias work at local early childhood conferences or hold a one-day conference or preconference day before your local, state, or regional AEYC conference.

6. Decide on membership criteria for the activist group. These criteria relate to your planning committee's vision of the purpose, goals and makeup of your activist group. It is advisable to keep the activist group size to approximately twenty people.

You may decide that you do not want to use selection criteria but instead will open the group to everyone who is interested. However, this may result in a group that does not balance the various cultural, early childhood, and diversity issues in your community. It will also more likely be a group that includes people who first need considerable cultural identity and anti-oppression work before they can begin to do this work with others—so it is less likely to be an activist or leadership group.

In the pilot CRAB project we identified both group and individual variables, because we wanted a group that was made up of people who reflected a variety of individual perspectives and who would be able to take on leadership tasks such as training, consulting, and organizing. We agreed that we would not include beginners in diversity and equity work, because we hoped that CRAB group members would be preparing themselves to work with these beginners as they began doing training. In addition, because we wanted to develop new leadership, we wanted a balance between grass roots people and individuals already in leadership positions in early childhood groups. These are the criteria we used for the group as a whole. Among group members, we wanted:

- a range of ethnic or cultural backgrounds;
- a range of early childhood work;
- a range of diversity/equity work (for example, cultural/anti-racism, disability rights, gay and lesbian rights, and so on);
- connections with community-based groups as well as early childhood system programs; and
- additional identity diversity such as gender, disability, sexual orientation, and class.

We used these criteria for individual members. We wanted each CRAB group participant to have:

- a sense of one's cultural identity;
- at least a beginning awareness of institutional racism or other oppressions;
- evidence of a sense of personal responsibility for creating social change; and
- a readiness to become more visible leaders and trainers.

7. Decide on an application process. Develop questions that will give you information about people that will enable you to make selections based on the criteria you have identified. Consider several ways people can respond to the application in addition to writing. For example, oral interviews done individually or in small groups by people with whom applicants feel comfortable, or a written or oral application in the language in which the individual is most comfortable.

We used a five-tiered sorting framework to make decisions after applications came in order to create the group makeup we wanted. It included looking at each applicant's:

- responses to our application questions;
- identity background;
- experience with various kinds of diversity/equity work;
- role in early childhood education; and
- grass roots or organizational leadership experience.

We learned that it wasn't a good idea to accept "loners"—people known for being very individualistic or with no connections to groups in the early childhood community or their cultural community.

8. Choose group co-coordinators. We found that the group coordinator plays an essential role in the success of the group at every stage of its development. While the operating principle of the group is collaboration—where every voice is equally important and everyone learns from one another—effective leadership within the group keeps it on track and moving forward through the various ups and downs of the group

dynamics and challenges of the work with others. The group coordinators may come out of the planning committee and may be the person or people who began the process, but do not assume that either of these situations will be the case.

We recommend that the planning committee consider the following criteria when choosing group coordinators:

Co-coordinators rather than a single coordinator
A team of two brings different perspectives and skills to work, offers a wider range of connections within the early childhood and other communities, and provides essential support to one another for dealing with group and individual issues as they arise.

Diversity in cultural backgrounds and/or other kinds of diversity work in the arenas you most want to affect
For example, if your primary focus is the early childhood system, then at least one co-coordinator should be from that arena. However, it may be beneficial not to limit both co-coordinator positions to people in early childhood but also to consider people in allied fields or community work related to children or parent leaders.

Individuals with an organizing perspective and experience who have strong connections to the fields and communities with whom you want to work
However, we advise not selecting individuals already in top leadership positions within early childhood or other human services because doing so ties the group too closely to the established system that you want to change.

The skills needed by co-coordinators
We found the following skills to be essential:

- ◆ demonstrated commitment to the work;
- ◆ an ability to listen to others without putting her own perspective in the way;
- ◆ demonstrated community or grass roots organizing ability;

- self-awareness and understanding of one's ethnic and cultural identity and one's group position within the power dynamics of racism and other systemic power relationships;
- an awareness of the phases of group dynamics in a diverse group and an ability to facilitate a diverse group;
- willingness to allow the group's agenda to emerge rather than impose one's own agenda;
- patience and persistence; and
- sense of humor.

Training

While a co-coordinator's life and work should provide evidence of at least the beginnings of the skills mentioned above, these can be further developed and strengthened by participating in training focused on building the capacity to coordinate groups. Training institutes (national or regional) are in the planning stages during the writing of this book.

9. Seek local funding to support the group's work. The planning committee may want to set up a network of individuals willing to help the group get funds to start and then maintain itself. Such funding may be used to support the following:

- leadership training for group coordinators (funds could also be used to buy a piece of their time so they don't have to do coordinating tasks on top of a full time job);
- phone, copying, postage costs;
- child care or substitute pay;
- mileage to meetings;
- food for meetings;
- accessibility to physical location and to information for people with disabilities—for example, getting materials put on tape or in Braille;
- translation equipment or interpreters;
- resource library for group members; and
- retreat costs: room and board, additional trainers, child care as needed.

Look for both direct and in-kind funding sources. For example, explore relationships with local foundations and individual donors; look for in-kind support such as meeting space, copying, phone mailings, and technical assistance for fund-raising; and consider contributions from group members such as from the honoraria for training workshops and consulting jobs connected to the group's work.

Be very thoughtful about fund-raising. Sometimes the criteria for funding from a particular foundation or other source may limit or take you away from your vision, goals, or operating principles. Moreover, most foundation funding is limited by the foundation's rules, not by the needs of our work. Therefore, other more long-term sources of funding are also necessary—such as individual donors, local or state early childhood organizations, state education funds, and local foundations that support long-term projects. Ultimately, don't let the funding source drive your work.

GUIDELINE 5: Connect with Our National Network

We are in the process of setting up a national network of early childhood cultural democracy and social justice activist groups whose members will be able to support one another through exchanging analysis, strategies, and personal experiences; sharing one another's expertise in specific areas; communicating through newsletters, e-mail, and chat groups; and meeting at regional and national conferences. The national network will also have ties internationally with other groups doing similar work in other countries. Once you form your group, you will have access to this network. Our warmest wishes are with you as you embark on your organizing adventure. For technical assistance and training to set up an early childhood activist group, get in touch with Louise Derman-Sparks at Pacific Oaks College, 5 Westmoreland Place, Pasadena, CA 91103-3592 (Phone: 626-397-1306; 818-397-1300. Fax: 626-798-1907; 626-797-1907. E-mail: rldsparks@aol.com).

Resources

The following list of resources focuses on adult issues. It is only a beginning. There are many more books in existence and new ones that need to be written about what it means for adults to take on the challenges discussed in this book. You will find other references in the books listed here. These resources are intended for your own education and to use with other adults. For further resources and information, consult such sources as the Teaching for Change catalog (available from Network of Educators on the Americas, PO Box 73038, Washington, DC 20056-3038).

History and Institutional Dynamics of Oppression

Albelda, Randy. *The War on the Poor: A Defense Manual*. Boston: New Press, 1996. Facts and analysis about the economy, employment, gender roles and family, and the myths about welfare.

Amott, Teresa, and Julie Matthaei. *Race, Gender, and Work: A Multicultural Economic History of Women in the United States*. Boston: South End Press, 1991. A useful book for placing the economic realities of early childhood into a larger context, one that is rarely included in economic histories.

Barndt, Joseph. *Dismantling Racism: The Continuing Challenge to White America*. Minneapolis: Augsburg Fortress, 1991. Written with a Christian audience in mind, the discussion of the various forms of racism and whites' role in dismantling it are very useful whatever one's religious beliefs.

Blumenfeld, William, ed. *Homophobia: How We All Pay the Price*. Boston: Beacon Press, 1992. A range of essays that counter myths, provide useful information, and help us understand why everyone pays a price for discrimination against gays and lesbians. Provides ideas for an anti-homophobia workshop.

Ending Racism: Working for a Racism Free 21st Century. Crossroads, 1996. Videocassette. An introduction to the concepts of institutional racism, the impact of ending legal segregation, and where we still need to go to dismantle systemic racism. A multiethnic group discusses these issues. Available from Crossroads Milwaukee, 2218 North 36th Street, Milwaukee, WI 53208.

hooks, bell. *Yearning: Race, Gender, and Cultural Politics.* Boston: South End Press, 1990. Forceful essays by one of our most brilliant African American thinkers that integrate gender and race issues in ways not often encountered.

————. *Killing Rage: Ending Racism.* New York: Holt, 1994. Essays that describe the roles of both whites and people of color in creating what hooks calls "beloved community" and the barriers that stand in our way.

Kivel, Paul. *Uprooting Racism: How White People Can Work for Racial Justice.* Philadelphia: New Society Press, 1996. Analysis of individual, cultural, and institutional racism that also includes many useful experiential exercises. One particular contribution is a chapter on anti-Semitism and the role for Jewish people in the struggle to dismantle racism.

Spring, Joel H. (1997). *Deculturalization and the Struggle for Equality: A Brief History of the Struggle of Dominated Cultures in the United States,* 2d ed. New York: McGraw-Hill. A discussion of how cultural racism impacts ethnic groups not part of the dominant culture and the role of resisting cultural loss in the struggle against racism.

Takaki, Ronald. *A Different Mirror: A History of Multicultural America.* Boston: Little, Brown, 1993. An account of U.S. history from the perspective of Native Americans, African Americans, Asian Americans, Irish Americans, Jewish Americans, Latino Americans, and others. By viewing U.S. history through a lens that is not Eurocentric, the author explores the fundamental question of what it means to be an American.

Zinn, Howard. *A People's History of the United States.* New York: Harper, 1980. A very readable history that looks at U.S. history from the perspective of the working people—women as well as men—of all ethnic groups that built this country. These facts are rarely found in history textbooks.

Resistance

Aguilar-San Juan, Karen, ed. *The State of Asian American Activism and Resistance in the 1990s.* Boston: South End Press, 1994.

Apthker, Herbert. *Anti-Racism in U.S. History: The First Two Hundred Years.* Westport, CT: Praeger, 1993.

Golden, Renny. *Dangerous Memories: Invasion and Resistance Since 1492.* CRTF-CA, 1991. Stories of 500 years of African American and indigenous resistance against oppression in the Americas. Available from Teaching for Change Catalog, Network of Educators on the Americas, PO Box 73038, Washington, DC 20056-3038.

Salt of the Earth. Produced by Paul Jarrico and directed by H. Biberman, 1951. Film. A film that depicts a copper miner's strike in the Southwest and the interconnected dynamics of class, race, and gender. Both professional actors and actresses and the people actually involved in the strike make up the cast.

Moraga, Cherrie, and Gloria Anzaldua, eds. *This Bridge Called My Back: Writings by Radical Women of Color.* New York: Kitchen Table Women of Color Press, 1983. A wonderful collection of poems, essays, and short stories that provides an important perspective on the lives and feelings of women of color.

Nabokov, Peter, ed. *Native American Testimony: A Chronicle of Indian–White Relations from Past to Present.* New York: Penguin, 1991.

Community Organizing

Barndt, Deborah. *Naming the Moment: Political Analysis for Action: A Manual for Community Groups.* Toronto, Canada: The Jesuit Centre, 1989. An introduction to a four-phase approach to political analysis with examples of how groups have used it to analyze their own issues. Available from Doris Marshall Institute, 64 Charles Street East, Toronto M4Y 1T1, Canada.

Cunningham, Frank, et al. *Social Movements/Social Change: The Politics and Practice of Organizing.* Toronto, Canada: Between the Lines, 1988. A framework and practical ideas for doing community organizing.

Kahn, Si. (1982) *Organizing: A Guide for Grassroots Leaders.* New York: McGraw-Hill. A framework and practical ideas for helping community groups gain and strengthen community organizing skills.

Soto, Lourdes Diaz. *Language, Culture, and Power: Bilingual Families and the Struggle for Quality Education.* New York: State University of New York Press, 1997. A powerful account of how families in an urban setting struggled to gain the kind of bilingual education they believed necessary for their children.

Stroup, Nibs, and Inez Fleming. *While We Run This Race: Confronting the Power of Racism in a Southern Church.* Maryknoll, NY: Orbis Press, 1995. A first-hand account by an interracial team of experiences working with others to transform their church. The lessons have meaning for anyone working for community change.

Identity Development and Adult Education Strategies

Arnold, Rick, Bev Bureke, Carl James, D'Arcy Martin, and Barb Thomas. *Educating for a Change.* Toronto, Canada: Between the Lines and the Doris Marshall Institute for Education and Action, 1995. A resource guide for doing interactive workshops on various aspects of social change that includes a conceptual framework as well as many specific techniques.

Bisson, Julie. *Celebrate! An Anti-Bias Guide to Enjoying Holidays in Early Childhood Programs.* St. Paul: Redleaf Press, 1997. Guidelines for discussing one of the hot issues in anti-bias education—the use of holiday celebrations in programs for young children.

Boal, Augusto. *Games for Actors and Non Actors.* New York: Routledge, 1996. A collection of interactive exercises and games that build trust and communication and bring fun into workshops and classes on educational and social change.

Carter, Margie, and Deb Curtis. *Training Teachers: A Harvest of Theory and Practice.* St. Paul: Redleaf Press, 1994. A guidebook for constructivist and transformative training of early childhood practitioners that weaves cultural and anti-bias issues throughout. This book also includes a strong section on doing culturally relevant and anti-bias training.

Derman-Sparks, Louise, and Carol Brunson Phillips. *Teaching/Learning Anti-Racism: A Developmental Approach.* New York: Teachers College Press, 1997. Examines the developmental phases that adults experience as they grapple with understanding institutional racism and what it means to construct anti-racist consciousness and behavior. The weekly activities of a semester-long class at Pacific Oaks College and the instructor's reflections on the challenges of teaching provide a context in which to view the students' growth.

Horton, Myles, and Paulo Freire. *We Make the Road by Walking.* Philadelphia: Temple University Press, 1990. A conversation between two pioneering leaders of transformative education who forged the path for educators wanting to connect teaching and social change.

Katz, Judith M. *White Awareness: A Handbook for Anti-Racism Training*. Norman: University of Oklahoma Press, 1978. Based on the author's experience working with white groups, numerous useful activities are described in detail and placed within the arenas of change necessary for developing white anti-racist consciousness and behavior.

Tatum, Beverly Daniels. *Why Are All the Black Kids Sitting Together in the Cafeteria? And Other Conversations About Race.* New York: Harper, 1997. The author offers a detailed explanation of developing racial and cultural identity for people of color and whites. A must read for anyone working for educational social change in the areas of cultural relevancy and racism.

Thompson, Becky, and Sangeeta Tyagi. *Names We Call Home.* New York: Routledge, 1996. Personal narratives written by people of color and whites that explore how to grapple with forming cultural identity while understanding the context of a systemically racist society. The narratives are also useful for helping others uncover their own often buried identity struggles.

York, Stacey. *Developing Roots and Wings: A Trainer's Guide to Affirming Culture in Early Childhood Programs.* St. Paul: Redleaf Press, 1992. Numerous activities for doing workshops with early childhood practitioners, particularly beginners on diversity and bias teaching.

Also from Redleaf Press

All the Colors We Are: The Story of How We Get Our Skin Color
by Katie Kissinger, with photos by Wernher Krutein. Outstanding full-color photographs showcase the beautiful diversity of human skin color and offer children a simple, accurate explanation of how we are the color we are.

Roots and Wings: Affirming Culture in Early Childhood Programs
by Stacey York. A unique approach to multicultural education that helps shape positive attitudes toward cultural differences. Includes over 60 activities for increasing children's understanding of differences.

**Developing Roots and Wings: A Trainer's Guide to Affirming Culture
in Early Childhood Programs**
by Stacey York. Everything you need to offer high-quality multicultural training. Includes over 170 training activities and more than 50 time-saving handouts.

Training Teachers: A Harvest of Theory and Practice
by Margie Carter and Deb Curtis. Help teachers experience constructing their own knowledge and respecting their own learning styles so they can help children do the same. Some of the best ideas in teaching and learning are put into action with these innovative training tools.

Celebrate! An Anti-Bias Guide to Enjoying Holidays in Early Childhood Programs
by Julie Bisson, with a preface by Louise Derman-Sparks. Filled with strategies for implementing holiday activities that are exciting, not biased, and developmentally appropriate.

We All Belong: Multicultural Child Care That Works
by the Australian Early Childhood Association. Turn cultural diversity into a powerful, creative force. Learn the principles that transformed this Australian center into a stimulating place where everyone feels at home. Ideal for staff training and program planning. User's guide included. Video, 20 min.

The Kindness Curriculum: Introducing Young Children to Loving Values
by Judith Anne Rice. Over 60 imaginative, exuberant activities that create opportunities for kids to practice kindness, empathy, conflict resolution, respect, and more.

Making It Better: Activities for Children Living in a Stressful World
by Barbara Oehlberg. This important book offers bold new information about the physical and emotional effects of stress, trauma, and violence on children today and gives teachers and caregivers the confidence to help children survive, thrive, and learn.

Reflecting Children's Lives: A Handbook for Planning Child-Centered Curriculum
by Deb Curtis and Margie Carter. A practical guide to help you put children and childhood at the center of your curriculum. Rethink and refresh your ideas about scheduling, observations, play, materials, space, and emergent themes.

To order or for a free catalog call
1-800-423-8305